MAR 2 8 2011

Magic Johnson

ATHLETE

Black Americans of Achievement

LEGACY EDITION

Muhammad Ali

Maya Angelou

Josephine Baker

George Washington Carver

Ray Charles

Johnnie Cochran

Bill Cosby

Frederick Douglass

W.E.B. Du Bois

Jamie Foxx

Aretha Franklin

Marcus Garvey

Savion Glover

Alex Haley

Jimi Hendrix

Gregory Hines

Langston Hughes

Jesse Jackson

Magic Johnson

Scott Joplin

Coretta Scott King

Martin Luther King Jr.

Spike Lee

Malcolm X

Bob Marley

Thurgood Marshall

Barack Obama

Jesse Owens

Rosa Parks

Colin Powell

Condoleezza Rice

Chris Rock

Will Smith

Clarence Thomas

Sojourner Truth

Harriet Tubman

Nat Turner

Madam C.J. Walker

Booker T. Washington

Oprah Winfrey

Stevie Wonder

Tiger Woods

Black Americans of Achievement
LEGACY EDITION

Magic Johnson

ATHLETE

David Aretha

CHELSEA HOUSE
PUBLISHERS
An imprint of Infobase Publishing

Magic Johnson

Chelsea House
An imprint of Infobase Publishing
132 West 31st Street
New York, NY 10001

Library of Congress Cataloging-in-Publication Data

Aretha, David.
Magic Johnson : athlete / by David Aretha. — Legacy ed.
     p.   cm. — (Black Americans of achievement)
Includes bibliographical references and index.
ISBN 978-1-60413-684-5 (hardcover)
1. Johnson, Earvin, 1959–   —Juvenile literature. 2. Basketball players—United States—Biography—Juvenile literature. I. Title. II. Series.
GV884.J63A74 2010
796.323092—dc22   [B]   2009050607

Chelsea House books are available at special discounts when purchased in bulk quantities for businesses, associations, institutions, or sales promotions. Please call our Special Sales Department in New York at (212) 967-8800 or (800) 322-8755.

You can find Chelsea House on the World Wide Web at http://www.chelseahouse.com.

Text design by Keith Trego
Cover design by Keith Trego
Composition by Keith Trego
Cover printed by Bang Printing, Brainerd, MN
Book printed and bound by Bang Printing, Brainerd, MN
Date printed: August 2010
Printed in the United States of America

10 9 8 7 6 5 4 3 2 1

This book is printed on acid-free paper.

All links and Web addresses were checked and verified to be correct at the time of publication. Because of the dynamic nature of the Web, some addresses and links may have changed since publication and may no longer be valid.

Contents

A Magical Moment

Just one more game. That's all Magic Johnson wanted to play. Just one more chance to trade shots with Michael Jordan, run the floor with Isiah Thomas, and brighten the arena with his million-dollar smile.

On November 7, 1991, the Los Angeles Lakers superstar had retired from the National Basketball Association (NBA) at age 32 after announcing he had contracted HIV, the virus that causes AIDS. Showing their devotion, fans elected the retired player to the NBA All-Star Game, scheduled for February 9, 1992. Johnson wanted to play. It could be, he thought, his last hurrah.

But then came the backlash.

Some NBA players did not want to share the court with Magic. They feared they would contract the dreaded virus, which at the time was considered a death sentence. What if they bumped up against his sweaty body? What if Johnson cut

Earvin "Magic" Johnson announces his retirement from the Los Angeles Lakers at a press conference while (*from left to right*) NBA Commissioner David Stern and former teammate Kareem Abdul-Jabbar look on. Johnson retired on November 7, 1991, after learning he had tested positive for HIV.

himself and they touched his blood? Would that cause them to get HIV? They were unsure, and they did not want to take the chance.

Magic Johnson, some players believed, should be banned from the court for life.

NBA Commissioner David Stern allowed Johnson to play, but it was a much-debated issue. Stern talked about consulting "with league medical advisors" and how Magic's presence "should not pose any health risk to Magic or the other participants."

That January, Australian players worried about possibly facing Johnson in that summer's Olympic Games. According to the Associated Press, Dr. Brian Sando announced: "I would certainly recommend that our basketballers [the Australian Olympic team] not compete with a team of which Magic Johnson was a member. That risk—even though it's small—you cannot absolutely say it's never going to occur."

It all seemed so wrong. After all, this was Magic Johnson, the five-time NBA champion who had rejuvenated the league with his infectious enthusiasm. Johnson had brought "Showtime" to the L.A. Forum and added "winning time" to the sports lexicon.

Johnson was determined to play in the All-Star Game, largely to support those with HIV and AIDS who had been shunned by society. The game would take place at the Orlando Arena, home of the Orlando Magic. As fellow players arrived that weekend, some were still apprehensive. But Isiah Thomas, the Detroit Pistons' star point guard, went out on a limb to support Johnson, his longtime friend.

"When some of the players decided that they did not want to play, I called a players' meeting," Thomas said, as noted on NBA.com. "I wanted to make sure all the players got out on the court and everyone dealt with it in a professional manner."

"SMILING AND DOING HIS THING"

The fear and tension, palpable throughout the week, dissipated by game time. Golden State guard Tim Hardaway, selected as a starter for the game, graciously allowed Johnson to start in his place. And when the starting lineups were announced, the crowd rose to its feet and showered Johnson with applause.

From that point on, it was just like every other All-Star Game, with Johnson dazzling the world with his spectacular play. "It was great seeing Magic back out on the floor, smiling and doing his thing," Thomas said in an NBA.com article. If his illness had affected his stamina, no one could tell. Johnson played more minutes than anyone else (29), while leading all players in points (25) and assists (nine).

With the game out of hand (Johnson's Western Conference would win 153-113), both teams allowed Thomas to go one-on-one against Johnson for old-time's sake. After Thomas missed his shot, Michael Jordan took his chances against his old nemesis, but his try rimmed out. "If this is going to be it for me," Johnson told the press after the game, "I wanted to get Isiah one more time and I wanted to get Michael one more time."

Finally, with the clock winding down, Johnson got the chance to launch one last shot. Taking a pass from Clyde Drexler, he attempted a three-pointer over Thomas. Nothing but net. The crowd went wild, and even with 14 seconds still to go, the players called it a day. In perhaps the most emotional moment in NBA history, players from both teams embraced Magic Johnson. They hugged him and slapped high-fives. Thomas handed him the game ball and kissed him on the cheek. Johnson was named the game's MVP.

"Words mean a lot, but it's feelings that count the most," Johnson told reporters after the game. "Ours is a game of compassion. I'll never forget those hugs and high-fives."

The game many had feared had turned into a memory that all would cherish. Don Nelson, the West's head coach, told the press after the game: "When you consider all the circumstances surrounding this game and what happened on the floor, it will be the highlight of my 2,500 games. It will go up there as No. 1 in my career."

Afterward, Johnson was all that anyone could talk about. "He went out the way he wanted to go out—with a lot of respect," Jordan said during the post-game interviews. "It was one of those things where he wanted to show everybody that he can still play, and not one time did I doubt that he could."

To the gathered reporters, Johnson called the game's final moments "the perfect ending to the story. I was trying to write this story all week, but I couldn't come up with an ending. That was like I was at my typewriter and said: 'Here's my ending.'"

Magic Johnson holds the NBA All-Star Game Most Valuable Player trophy, surrounded by his wife, Cookie Johnson (*center*), and his parents, Earvin Johnson Sr. and Christine Johnson, at the Orlando Arena on February 9, 1992.

Most important to Johnson, he was able to show to the world that people with HIV could still lead productive lives. "This game was to educate everybody," he told the press after the game, "and I think we got that across."

Anthony Sprauve, spokesman for AIDS Project Los Angeles, shared his feelings. "I found it very exciting and very emotional," Sprauve told an Associated Press reporter. "The message that this sends is that people with HIV should not be ostracized, they should not be shuffled away. They're around us, and they're part of our society, and we should welcome them."

Like NBA fans throughout the world, Commissioner Stern will never forget that special day in Orlando. "It was in all ways magical," he said, as quoted by NBA.com. "I smile every time I think about it."

2

Where the Magic Began

One of the most important days in Earvin Johnson's life occurred when he was nine years old, and it had nothing to do with basketball.

One Saturday, Earvin and his friends strolled into a neighborhood store in Lansing, Michigan, and decided to steal candy and balloons. Being the leader of the group (he has always been a leader), Earvin snatched the goods, and the boys sneaked out of the store without paying. Little did they realize that the woman behind the counter had witnessed the crime through a mirror in the upper corner of the store. Knowing it was Earvin, she called the Johnsons' residence and spoke to his mother, Christine.

When Earvin arrived home, his mother scolded him and sent him upstairs to wait for his father. Oh no, the boy thought. He never wanted to upset his dad. Earvin Sr. worked around the clock to support 10 children, and "Big E" did not have the patience for such behavior.

Earvin's heart pounded when he heard his father ascend the stairs, and he cried when Dad entered the room. Without a word, his father took off his belt, put the boy over his knee, and whipped his behind. Earvin sobbed, but, as he recalled in his first autobiography, *Magic*, it "really didn't hurt that much."

"Why'd you do it, Junior?" Dad asked.

Earvin could come up with no good reason, except that he was showing off to his friends.

"Listen, Junior," Dad said, "you don't have to steal. If you want something, tell me. I'll get it for you. If I can't, then you know you can do without. Understand?"

Earvin nodded through his tears.

"You don't have to be stealing," Dad preached. "That'll only get you into trouble, and you're too smart for that." Earvin started to feel better. "Come on," Dad said. "Get dressed. Let's go out to the racetrack."

Earvin Jr. and Sr. loved watching the drag races together. They ate hot dogs, chatted about the cars, and jumped up and down when the dragsters whizzed by. On the car rides home, Earvin often fell asleep on his dad's lap. They had a great time at the races on this evening, too. As for the day's earlier event: "My father never mentioned the incident again," Johnson wrote in *Magic*, "he didn't have to."

This story has less to do with crime and punishment than it does with love and family. And as a child, Earvin had lots of love and lots of family.

A FULL HOUSE

Born on August 14, 1959, Earvin Johnson Jr. was the fourth of Earvin and Christine's seven children. Siblings Quincy, Larry, and Pearl were older, and three girls came later—Kim and the twins, Evelyn and Yvonne. In addition, Earvin Sr. had fathered three other children before he married Christine.

Those children lived in the South and sometimes came to visit, which added to the general chaos in a house that had only one bathroom.

Nevertheless, Earvin cherishes his boyhood memories. The Johnsons lived in a yellow, three-bedroom frame house on Middle Street in an African-American neighborhood in Lansing. Many of the men in the area worked for General Motors or one of the automobile company's subsidiaries. The adults were mostly hardworking, churchgoing folks, and their children loved to play outside. Earvin knew many of the kids in the neighborhood. He saw them at school, church, the Boys Club, and, of course, on the Main Street basketball courts, just two blocks from his house.

More than anything, Earvin loved to play basketball. In the summer after second grade, his mother awoke one morning to realize that Junior was not in the house. He had gotten up early and left for the courts without telling anybody. From then on, Earvin had to wake his mom and tell her he was leaving. The crack-of-dawn farewell became a morning ritual.

Earvin dribbled his basketball everywhere—to the courts, to the grocery store, and inside the house. He dribbled down Middle Street in the early morning, prompting neighbors to scold him for waking them up. Even as a young tyke, he was a regular at the courts, playing before and after school and all day

IN HIS OWN WORDS...

In an interview quoted on the NBA's official Web site, Magic Johnson recalled:

> I practiced all day. I dribbled to the store with my right hand and back with my left. Then I slept with my basketball.

Source: http://www.nba.com/history/players/johnsonm_bio.html.

in the summer. In the winter, he shoveled away the snow so he could dribble and shoot. At night, he slept with his basketball.

When he was not playing the real thing, Earvin indulged in "sock ball," which he played by penciling a rectangle on the living room wall and firing balls of socks at his target. Sometimes he played against Larry and Evelyn, while other times he played alone. Whenever his mother could not find the twins' socks, she blamed Junior. Inevitably, the socks would be found wedged inside the sofa cushions or lying under the couch or chairs.

While Earvin dreamed of basketball glory, his father labored in the real world. From 4 P.M. to 1 A.M., Earvin Sr. operated the grinding boot on the Fisher Body assembly line, sometimes burning his clothes and skin. Then he worked a second job. For two and a half years, he pumped gas for seven hours a day. He later replaced that second job with his own business, in which he cleaned shops and hauled away rubbish.

Years later, Junior paid tribute to his dad. "My father is my idol, so I always did everything like him," Earvin said, as recounted in the book *My Soul Looks Back*. "He used to work two jobs and still come home happy every night. He didn't do drugs or drink, and he wouldn't let anyone smoke in his house. Those are rules I adopted, too."

Earvin Sr. had worked his whole life. As the son of a poor sharecropper in Mississippi, he toiled in the cotton and tobacco fields as a child, rarely getting a chance to go to school. While serving in the U.S. Army, he met Christine, who had grown up in tobacco country in North Carolina. They married while Earvin Sr. was still in the service and then settled down in Lansing.

According to Earvin Jr., Christine was often exhausted. She cleaned house, cared for the children, and for a while even worked a full-time job.

"Mother," Junior once told her, as recounted in *Magic*, "you're really tired, aren't you?"

"Yes, Junior, I am."

"Well, someday I'm going to become somebody and you won't ever have to work again."

His mother flashed a big smile, which always made young Earvin feel good.

"People talk about my smile," he wrote in *Magic*, "but hers is the original. It is as bright and warm as the sun at midday, and just seeing it perks me up."

Following their parents' example, the Johnson kids had a strong work ethic. Earvin Jr. did well in school and helped around the house by vacuuming, cooking, and washing dishes. He even earned his own money, raking leaves and shoveling snow in the neighborhood. But the Johnsons had plenty of fun, too. On Saturdays, they made pizzas, piling the pies with mushrooms, onions, and hamburger. They also watched a lot of TV together, with such programs as *Columbo*, *Sanford and Son*, and *The Flip Wilson Show* being among their favorites.

JUNIOR HIGH SENSATION

While Junior's father and some of his siblings were good at basketball, Junior was exceptional. When Earvin entered Dwight Rich Junior High School, he was a six-footer who could handle the ball and shoot the lights out. After scoring 26 points in a game, he was ecstatic to learn that he had been written about in the local newspaper. Earvin soon became the talk of the neighborhood, and Dad began asking for time off from work so that he could see his son in action. In one game, Earvin scored 48 points—phenomenal considering that quarters were only six minutes long and he did not play after the third quarter. By ninth grade, Earvin stood six feet five inches and seemed to dominate every game he played.

Johnson found some of his best competition on the neighborhood courts. His biggest rival was Jay Vincent, who lived on the east side of Lansing. (Earvin lived on the west side.) Within a few years, both would play for Michigan State and go on to the NBA. But in their early years, they battled on the playgrounds, in the Parks and Recreation League, and even in high school. When Earvin faced Jay, it was a major event.

Even though Earvin was already a budding star in junior high, several men helped him refine his game. He learned the art of rebounding from junior high coach Louis Brockhaus. In eighth and ninth grade, he developed his inside moves with the help of coach Paul Rosekrans. Earvin's father, a former high school player, showed him how to execute the running hook shot. In one-on-one games, Big E played "dirty"—pushing, banging, and grabbing his son to get an advantage. Dad was trying to impart a lesson: In the higher leagues, opponents would play rough, and Earvin would have to learn how to deal with the physical play.

Earvin also learned a lot by watching his idols, most of whom happened to be point guards. His dad took him to see Marques Haynes, the "World's Fastest Dribbler," a former Harlem Globetrotter who toured with the Harlem Magicians. Among NBA players, he marveled at Earl "The Pearl" Monroe, whose lightning-quick hands turned the ball into an orange blur.

Most of all, Earvin loved attending Detroit Pistons games at Cobo Arena in Detroit. Pistons point guard Dave Bing (who would later become Detroit's mayor) burned NBA opponents with laser-beam passes, dazzling drives to the basket, and net-ripping shots from the perimeter. If only I could be as good as Dave Bing, Earvin dreamed.

At age 11, Earvin got the chance to meet Lew Alcindor (who would soon change his name to Kareem Abdul-Jabbar) in Cobo's visitors' locker room. In only his second professional season, the seven-foot-two-inch Milwaukee Bucks center was already the best player in the NBA, averaging about 30 points and 16 rebounds per game. When it came time for Earvin to ask for his autograph, he was too awestruck to talk. Another kid had to ask for him. It is likely that neither the

Dave Bing of the Detroit Pistons (21) drives past Norm Van Lier (2) of the Chicago Bulls during the NBA playoffs in Chicago, Illinois, on April 5, 1974. As a kid, Earvin Johnson wished he could grow up to be as good as his hero, Dave Bing.

superstar nor the tongue-tied kid imagined that they would play on the same NBA team together for 10 seasons, winning five NBA championships.

As a teenager, Earvin only fantasized about playing in the NBA. He did not consider it a realistic goal. In fact, he always worried that the next level of competition would be difficult and that he had to continue to improve his game to be ready for that next challenge.

BLACK KID IN A WHITE SCHOOL

For as long as he could remember, Earvin had expected to attend Sexton High School, just five blocks from his house. Sexton, which boasted a dynamic basketball program, was a predominantly African-American school. Seemingly every kid in the neighborhood went there, until "busing" entered the equation.

In the 1970s, few government programs triggered as much controversy as busing. In 1954, the U.S. Supreme Court had ruled that segregation in public schools—with white students attending certain schools in a city and black students attending the others—was unconstitutional. Since white schools were almost always better funded than black schools, it was unfair to keep African-American students in poorer schools. In the 1970s, to counter the injustice, some cities forced school integration by busing black students to white schools and white students to black schools.

In general, students of both races did not like being bused to schools outside their neighborhoods. In 1974, Earvin was one of the African-American kids from his area who was selected to be bused to Everett High School, a mostly white public school several miles away. Earvin's parents opposed the decision. Their older sons, Quincy and Larry, had been bused to Everett and had witnessed brick throwing, fights, and other racial incidents. Earvin wrote a letter of appeal to the school board, but nothing came of it. He had to attend Everett High.

An example of school desegregation efforts can be seen in this photo taken in front of South Boston High School on September 24, 1974, showing black students arriving by bus at the mostly white school. This controversial program upset many students who were forced to endure it, including a young Earvin Johnson.

Earvin anticipated tensions at the new school. Years earlier, Everett basketball coach George Fox had cut Larry from the team—and race, Larry believed, had much to do with it. Because of the incident, Earvin was not looking forward to playing for Coach Fox. Moreover, because Earvin, then a sophomore, was so talented, the older players felt threatened.

Trouble erupted during the team's first scrimmage. On three successive plays, Earvin was wide open for an easy bucket and his teammate—a white senior—did not pass him the ball. After the third supposed snub, as Johnson later wrote in *Magic*, he yelled, "Give it up! I was wide open three straight times."

The player responded by shoving him and insulting him with a racial slur.

Coach Fox stepped in to make peace, but afterward Earvin was still fuming mad—uncharacteristic for the normally jovial teenager. Another player, a five-foot-three-inch white junior named Reggie Chastain, convinced Earvin to calm down and promised to talk to the coach. Reggie and Earvin became good friends, and even though the junior was not nearly as good a player as his younger teammate, Earvin held him in the highest esteem.

Earvin gradually adjusted to Everett High, even joining the school newspaper. His teammates valued his unselfish passing, and Coach Fox loosened up his formerly methodical offense to accommodate Earvin's creativity.

As a sophomore, Earvin turned a previously ordinary team into a powerhouse. Everett lost only one regular-season game and went all the way to the quarterfinals in the Class A (the

How Magic Got His Nickname

In his first game at Everett High School, Earvin Johnson scored only about a dozen points. In a game against Jackson Parkside High, however, not only did he score 36 points, but he grabbed 18 rebounds and tallied 16 assists. After the game, reporter Fred Stabley of the *Lansing State-Journal* asked Johnson if he could give him a nickname . . . perhaps "Magic"? Earvin said he was okay with it, and the next day Earvin "Magic" Johnson was written in type for the first time.

"I always tell people someone else would have came up with the nickname if I hadn't," Stabley said. "He was already going to be a special, magical person."

Earvin's mother, a devoutly religious woman, did not like the vanity of the nickname. His father told him that with a name like Magic, he would have a lot to live up to. But Earvin, who loved challenges, accepted the nickname and all that went with it. And he really had little choice, since pretty soon sportswriters and fans referred to him as Magic all the time.

highest level) state tournament. Everett lost that game due in part to Earvin's mental blunder. He called a timeout with 10 seconds remaining even though his Vikings had no timeouts remaining, which meant the other team got possession. He cried after the loss.

As a junior during the 1975-1976 season, Earvin became a statewide sensation. In a preseason road game against Detroit Northwestern, he put on a show for the big-city media, amassing the unheard-of totals of 40 points, 35 rebounds, and 20 assists. Against Sexton High, he scored 54 points, setting a record for a Lansing player.

Nevertheless, Earvin had plenty of reasons to remain humble. On Saturdays, he had to wake up early and help his father work. His grades slipped in school, forcing him to attend summer classes. On the court before his junior year, he played against George Gervin, one of the deadliest scorers in the NBA during the 1970s. As the "Ice Man" repeatedly blew by him, Johnson knew he had a long way to go to become NBA ready.

WINNING FOR REGGIE

Everett lost in the state semifinals in 1976, but Earvin experienced a much greater loss that summer. Earvin and Reggie Chastain had become the closest of friends. More than just teammates, they went to parties together and often drove to Jackson, Michigan, where they each had a girlfriend. One day that summer, the two friends had planned to ride to Jackson together, but Earvin had to bow out at the last minute. The next morning, Reggie's brother called Earvin with tragic news: Reggie had been killed on the road, the victim of a drunken driver.

"This was my first experience with death, and it was devastating," Johnson wrote in his second autobiography, *My Life*. "Everybody loved Reggie, this scrappy little fighter who not only made the team, but became a starter. He had so much heart. He feared nobody. And he taught me about courage when I really needed to learn it."

For Earvin, Reggie's death was like losing a member of his family. He would mourn his loss for months and would think about him during the big events in his life.

The Everett basketball team dedicated the 1976-1977 season to Reggie, and "Magic"—as Earvin had become known—raised his game to a higher level. The senior superstar scored so much early in the season (about 45 points per game) that Coach Fox told him that he had to pass more. His teammates had turned into spectators; they needed to be more involved. He responded by becoming more of a playmaker, and he quarterbacked the team all the way to the Class A state championship game.

Televised throughout the state, the game pitted Everett against a strong Brother Rice team at Crisler Arena in Ann Arbor. Everett led by two points with time running out when Brother Rice star Kevin Smith banked in a half-court shot at the buzzer. Fortunately for Everett, the game predated the three-point era. Otherwise, it would have been another heart-breaking tournament exit for the Vikings.

When the game entered overtime, Magic Johnson took over. He scored the first eight points of OT before fouling out with three minutes to go. After playing in his shadow for so long, his teammates got the chance to win on their own. They hung on for a 62-56 victory.

While the Vikings celebrated in the locker room, Earvin walked alone into a dark hallway. With tears in his eyes, he honored the spirit of Reggie. "We did it, man," he wrote in *My Life*. "You said we could, and we did. We did it for you."

3

National Champion

During his sophomore year of high school, Earvin Johnson was elated. Everett High coach George Fox presented him with letters from several colleges. Coaches at those schools wanted the young phenomenon to play basketball for their teams—he was being recruited! He could not wait to get home and tell his parents.

Johnson did not realize at the time, however, that those letters were the beginning of a nightmare. Up through his senior season, he would be hounded, pressured, and even subtly bribed to attend colleges across the country.

There has always been something unsettling about the recruiting process, especially when it comes to superstar players. College coaches—grown men and respected leaders—put on their best face in order to charm 17-year-olds into attending their schools. Sometimes the coaches are desperate; they need star talent to maintain their jobs. Other times it is about greed: The coach who accumulates the most talent can achieve fame and riches. Recruiting is often more about the coach and his program and not the student athlete—a lesson that Johnson quickly learned.

By his senior year, Johnson's phone rang from morning to night, even after the family changed its number. The head coaches and assistant coaches who called were pleasant, but Johnson and his parents always questioned their sincerity. His mother was skeptical of everyone who sent her flowers. A couple of recruiters offered money, which infuriated Earvin Sr. Will Jones, an assistant coach at Maryland, was among the most persistent recruiters. He hung around Lansing for long periods of time trying to woo Johnson.

Indiana University's Bobby Knight, one of the best coaches in the country, sat down with Johnson. Although Knight impressed Johnson with his straightforward talk and emphasis on education, the high school superstar did not like his rigid offense and his reputation as a hothead. Johnson then considered such schools as Maryland, UCLA, Notre Dame, and North Carolina, but he realized that he wanted to stay close to home. In the end, it came down to a choice between the University of Michigan (located in Ann Arbor, 65 miles [104.6 kilometers] southeast of Lansing) and Michigan State University (next door in East Lansing).

The University of Michigan was better academically, and its basketball team under coach Johnny Orr had reached the NCAA Finals in 1976 (against Indiana). But on his visit to Ann Arbor, Johnson picked up some vibes of resentment from a couple of Michigan's established players—just like what had happened when he joined the Everett team.

As for Michigan State, the Spartans had had a losing 12-15 season in 1976-1977 under new coach Jud Heathcote. Highstrung and prone to vocal outbursts, Heathcote was known to pound his forehead when particularly frustrated. While Johnson did not like hotheaded coaches, he realized that Heathcote was not so bad once he got to know him.

Always a sentimental guy, Johnson kept thinking how nice it would be to go to school near his hometown. Moreover, after an all-star tour in Germany, a large crowd of Michigan State fans greeted Johnson at the Lansing airport. They handed him a petition signed by 5,000 Lansing schoolchildren asking him to play at MSU—a gesture far more welcoming than the cold shoulder he had received in Ann Arbor.

Days later, Coach Fox organized a press conference at Everett High School. Reporters from across the state and country waited anxiously for Johnson's announcement. "I have decided to attend Michigan State University," he said. His supporters erupted in applause. "I don't think I could have gone anywhere else," he said, as he recalled in *Magic.* "I was born to be a Spartan."

RESURRECTING THE SPARTANS

Basketball season didn't start until late in the semester, so for a while Earvin was just like every other Michigan State student. In his dormitory, he roomed with Jay Vincent, his longtime friend and rival. Unlike some other superstar athletes, Johnson took academics seriously. He majored in telecommunications, minored in education, and maintained a B average. Though everyone sensed that he would make millions in the NBA, he also took a part-time job. For two nights a week, he worked as a disc jockey at a local disco. "EJ the DJ," they called him.

MSU students believed Magic Johnson would resurrect the university's basketball program. Johnson could feel the pressure from the beginning, when more students attended practices than fans had attended games in previous years. He began the season as the Spartans' point guard—the hardest position to learn, especially for a freshman. Along the way, he learned to adjust to the bigger, stronger competitors as well as the physical nature of Big Ten basketball. Coach Heathcote added to the tension with his endless yelling. He screamed at players for every little thing, especially if they committed a mental error.

Michigan State University's Earvin Johnson (33) makes one of his amazing passes over Illinois's Audie Matthews (43) in Big Ten action on February 25, 1978. Johnson's time on the Spartans helped revive the team's fortunes.

Johnson dealt with the vocal abuse better than others, since he too expected a lot from himself and his teammates.

In the first game of his freshman season, Johnson struggled, committing way too many turnovers and missing most of his shots. But it was not long before he caught up and surpassed the competition. Heathcote was a big help, working with Johnson on his jump shot, free-throw shooting, and defense. As the point guard, Johnson was Heathcote's coach on the floor, and the two were perfectly in sync. Johnson believed in his coach's five keys to victory: teamwork, defense, high-percentage shooting, offensive execution, and fast break.

Johnson and junior forward Greg Kelser, a tremendous leaper, ran the break to perfection. When Johnson alley-ooped a pass to Kelser for a rim-rattling dunk, the Spartans' home court, Jenison Fieldhouse, would erupt in cheers. Johnson, Kelser, and company did indeed resurrect the MSU program. The Spartans finished the 1977-1978 regular

Magic Johnson's College Statistics

Year	Team	G	FGM	FGA	FG%	FTM	FTA	FT%
1977-1978	MSU	30	175	382	.458	161	205	.785
1978-1979	MSU	32	173	370	.468	202	240	.842
Career		62	348	752	.463	363	445	.816

Year	Team	REB	AST	PTS	RPG	APG	PPG
1977-1978	MSU	237	222	511	7.9	7.4	17.0
1978-1979	MSU	234	269	548	7.3	8.4	17.1
Career		471	491	1,059	7.6	7.9	17.1

Key: G (games), FGM (field goals made), FGA (field goals attempted), FG% (field goal percentage), FTM (free throws made), FTA (free throws attempted), FT% (free throw percentage), REB (rebounds), AST (assists), PTS (points), RPG (rebounds per game), APG (assists per game), PPG (points per game).

season at 22-4. Moreover, their 15-3 record in the Big Ten earned them their first conference championship in 11 years. Johnson had lived up to the hype, earning the Associated Press Third Team All-America honors—an incredible achievement for a freshman.

Despite the sudden success, Johnson remained remarkably humble. He often went home on the weekends to eat, do laundry, and see his family. On Saturday nights, however, he found it hard to keep his ego in check, as young women swarmed around the charming superstar. One evening at a disco, Johnson was unable to keep his eyes off Earletha "Cookie" Kelly, a beautiful MSU freshman who lit up the dance floor. He took her out on his first-ever formal date (he even wore a suit), and Earvin and Earletha became an item.

Cookie was surprised that Johnson had not let his success go to his head. "I thought that he might be a showoff, but he wasn't like that at all," she wrote in *My Life*. "When he took me home, he acted like a real gentleman. I was shocked. I didn't expect that this popular athlete would be so respectful."

Magic and Cookie would endure a rocky relationship that first year and frequently got into heated arguments. One day, he took his anger out on the Michigan Wolverines, whipping them badly in Ann Arbor. But he was crazy about Cookie, the woman he would one day marry.

The nation at large got to know Magic Johnson in the 1978 NCAA Tournament. Back then, only 32 teams were invited, and the Spartans won their first two games with ease. Triumphs over Providence (77-63) and Western Kentucky (90-69) put them in the Elite Eight against Kentucky, the top team in the country. A victory would send them to the Final Four, where MSU had been only once (1957) in school history.

The Spartans stunned the Wildcats by taking a 31-24 lead with about 19 minutes left to play. But Heathcote's decision to slow the tempo proved unwise. Kentucky prevailed 52-49, with Johnson tallying just six points, five assists, and four rebounds.

Those numbers were far below his season averages of 17.0 points, 7.9 rebounds, and 7.4 assists.

THE ROAD TO THE FINAL FOUR

During the summer of 1978, Johnson experienced a whole new realm of stardom. He and a team of college all-stars traveled to the Soviet Union to face a talented team of Russians. As a tall African American in a nearly all-white country like the Soviet Union, he felt uncomfortable—especially with people gawking at him. He was glad to get home.

Before the summer was over, *Sports Illustrated* (*SI*) contacted Jud Heathcote. The editors planned to do a story on the top sophomore basketball players for the upcoming season and wanted to put Johnson on the cover. He was so excited that he could not sleep for three days. For the cover photo, he dunked a basketball while dressed in a tuxedo and top hat. "Michigan State's Classy Earvin Johnson," the cover stated.

In the cover story, "He's Gone to the Head of His Class," writer Larry Keith gushed over Johnson's unselfish, winning style of basketball:

> Johnson . . . is sure of what he will be doing: gliding down somebody's court, weaving in and out of traffic, frustrating his defensive man, checking the left and right lanes, waiting, waiting, waiting until just the right moment, and then—presto!—there it is, around his back, through his legs, side-arm, overhand, whatever sleight of hand it takes to get the ball to the right man in the right place at the right time.

In the article, Heathcote heaped praise on his star athlete. "In Earvin's case you don't talk about the points he scores," the coach said, "but the points he produces. Not just the baskets and assists, but the first pass that makes the second pass possible."

The *SI* cover vaulted Johnson to superstardom. Everywhere he went, he was hounded for autographs, yet he remained humble and maintained a team-first attitude. With Johnson, Kelser, and Vincent, the Spartans cruised through their early-season schedule in 1978-1979. By early January, they were ranked No. 1 in the country. But halfway through the season, it appeared that the sports world's two famous jinxes—the sophomore jinx and the *Sports Illustrated* cover jinx—might have struck the Magic Man.

In a span of two weeks, Michigan State lost three Big Ten games in the final seconds. Then came the shocker: an 18-point rout by Northwestern, a perennial doormat that had not won a conference game all season. Coach Heathcote met with his players afterward, asking them why they had been playing so poorly. It's the offense, they said. They needed to pick up the tempo. Heathcote agreed to let loose, and the players pledged to improve their intensity.

The rest of the season was like something out of a Hollywood movie. In their next game against Ohio State (which at the time was 8-0 in Big Ten games), Johnson suffered a badly sprained ankle. Yet, amid thunderous applause, he came back in the final minutes to lead the Spartans to victory. In the next game, on national television, MSU avenged its loss to Northwestern. The Spartans wound up winning 10 games in a row before losing the regular-season finale to Wisconsin on a 55-foot buzzer-beater.

Throughout the run, Johnson dazzled fans with his magical moves. "He can do things on the court that 6-foot-8 people aren't supposed to be able to do," wrote David Dupree in the *Washington Post*. "He is the best ballhandler and passer to appear in a long time and if he had a deadly jump shot to go with the rest of his game, he probably would be one of the greatest to ever play the sport."

Michigan State finished the regular season in a three-way tie for the Big Ten title at 13-5. In the NCAA Tournament, the

Indiana State forward Larry Bird is shown here in action against the Oklahoma Sooners during the NCAA Tournament on March 15, 1979. The rivalry between Bird and Magic Johnson would stretch into their NBA careers.

Spartans clicked on all cylinders. Seeded No. 2 in the Mideast Region, MSU opened with crushing victories over Lamar (95-64) and Louisiana State (71-57). In a marquee matchup against No. 1 seed Notre Dame, State prevailed 80-68 thanks to Kelser's 34 points. The Spartans had made it to the Final Four.

"I'm loving this, every minute of it," Johnson said at a press conference during Final Four week in Salt Lake City, Utah. "I'm like a kid going to a birthday party." Sky-high the whole week, the Spartans blew Pennsylvania out of the gym, winning 101-67. That set up a championship-game showdown against Indiana State, led by a player as exciting as Magic Johnson: Larry Bird.

SHOWDOWN: BIRD VS. MAGIC

Referred to as the "Hick from French Lick," Larry Bird had grown up poor in that small Indiana town. His alcoholic father committed suicide in 1975, and Bird dropped out of two colleges before settling at Indiana State. Though he was slow afoot and could not jump very high, the six-foot-nine-inch forward scored at will and hit open men with no-look passes. In three years at ISU, he averaged 30 points a game. Entering the 1979 NCAA championship game, his Sycamores were 33-0.

On March 26, 1979, sports fans across America geared up for the big game. They cared less about the teams than the individual matchup: Magic Johnson, the dazzling African American with the beaming smile vs. Larry Bird, the slow white guy who made magic of his own. That night, more than 35 million people viewed the game on NBC. To this day, it remains the most-watched NCAA championship game in history.

Early in the game, the Spartans took control. Bird never got on track, partially because of a broken left thumb and largely because of Michigan State's intense double-team. He sank just seven of 21 field goals as the Spartans cruised to a 75-64 victory. Johnson, who scored 24 points, punctuated the victory in the final seconds with a no-look, half-court lob to Kelser,

Magic Johnson of Michigan State celebrates his team's victory by cutting down the net after defeating Indiana State 75-64 to win the NCAA championship in Salt Lake City on March 26, 1979.

who slammed it home. "We have to get at least one play like that a game," Johnson told reporters afterward. "We wouldn't be Michigan State if we didn't."

Johnson and Kelser had led the Spartans to their first-ever national basketball championship. After the game, Johnson cut down the net while Bird cried in his towel. It was just the beginning of the two men's long and storied rivalry.

Upon the Spartans' return to East Lansing, thousands gathered for a raucous celebration. When Johnson was introduced, the crowd chanted, "Two more years! Two more years!" The cheering fans hoped that Johnson would delay his NBA dream and play his junior and senior seasons with MSU. With him in the lineup, the Spartans could challenge for the national title again. But "when Magic leaves," said Michigan coach Johnny Orr, as reported in the *Washington Post*, "they are going right back down where they were before he came."

"I don't know about two more years," Johnson told the crowd. "I don't know what I will do, but whatever it is, I hope you will continue to support me."

Those were not the words fans wanted to hear. To them, his response sounded like "See ya later . . . let's keep in touch." But the truth is, Johnson had yet to commit to the NBA. In his mind, it all depended on the flip of a coin.

4

Showtime!

Since 1985, basketball fans have eagerly awaited the annual NBA Lottery. The teams that did not make the previous season's playoffs are eligible, and the winner gets to choose first in the upcoming NBA Draft.

But before 1985, the NBA brass used a simpler "system" to determine who would get first pick. They flipped a coin. The team with the worst record in each conference participated, and the NBA commissioner's coin toss would determine the two teams' fate.

In 1979, the Chicago Bulls and the New Orleans Jazz were the worst teams in the Western Conference and Eastern Conference, respectively. Unfortunately for the Jazz, they had traded their 1979 first-round pick to the Los Angeles Lakers years earlier.

Johnson anxiously awaited the flip. In his mind, if Chicago won the toss, he would go back to Michigan State. The Bulls had never made it to the NBA Finals, and Johnson—who thrived on success—envisioned a gloomy future in Chicago. If the perennially strong Lakers won the toss, however, he would go to Los Angeles—but only if they offered enough money. If not, he would go back to school.

To complicate matters, the Lakers were unsure if they would select Johnson, even if they won the first overall pick. Although Larry Bird was unavailable (the Boston Celtics had drafted him in 1978), the Lakers liked shooting guard Sidney Moncrief and power forward David Greenwood. Los Angeles already had a terrific point guard in Norm Nixon, and scouts wondered whether Johnson could even make it as an NBA point guard. He was not especially quick, his jumper needed work, and he stood six feet nine inches—there had never been an NBA point guard that tall.

NBA Commissioner Larry O'Brien flipped a coin that came up tails, giving the Lakers the No. 1 pick. Team owner Jack Kent Cooke had been advised by his staff to draft Moncrief, but a further complication arose. Real estate magnate Jerry Buss was about to buy the Lakers (and the Los Angeles Kings in the National Hockey League) from Cooke, and Buss insisted that the Lakers draft Johnson. He was a winner, Buss believed, who would put fans in the seats. Cooke agreed to the demand; now he just had to convince Johnson to sign with the Lakers.

Cooke invited Johnson to Los Angeles to negotiate his potential salary. Magic brought his father, a lawyer, and his agent along with him. Cooke, a 66-year-old business tycoon from Canada, and the young athlete clashed immediately. For lunch, Cooke ordered Johnson a type of fish called sanddab, which Johnson could barely stomach. He also did not like Cooke's salary offer of $400,000. If he did not offer more, Johnson told Cooke, he would go back to school—and he was serious. While he liked the idea of playing for the Lakers, he was not eager to live so far from home. He also wanted to earn his college degree, either in the off-season or by returning to college full time.

Cooke came back with a $460,000-a-year offer, which Johnson rejected, and then $500,000, which he accepted. In the NBA Draft that June, the Lakers took Johnson No. 1. At age 19, he was on top of the world.

FROM LONELY ROOKIE TO NBA CHAMPION

That summer, the Johnson family shed plenty of tears. Magic cried on Lakers media day, when he first put on his L.A. jersey. His parents cried when he moved out of their Lansing house for good. And Johnson's eyes watered on the plane ride that took him to his new, faraway home.

Though he had been a big star in Lansing, Johnson felt small and lonely in Los Angeles. Intimidated by the enormous freeway system, he rarely strayed from his apartment. His teammates were older and had their own lives, and he wound up hanging out mostly with the team owner, Jerry Buss. Missing his old life, he spent endless hours on the phone with his family and friends.

On the court, Johnson stumbled in the early weeks of the 1979-1980 season. Before his first regular-season game, he tripped on his warm-up pants and fell on his face. When the Lakers' veteran center, Kareem Abdul-Jabbar, won the game

DID YOU KNOW?

Magic Johnson and Kareem Abdul-Jabbar frequently played each other in a basketball shooting game called H-O-R-S-E. The veteran usually won by sinking his trademark "sky hook." Johnson was so tired of losing to him in H-O-R-S-E that he insisted that Abdul-Jabbar teach him how to shoot the sky hook. Magic's version of it, dubbed the "baby hook," became a feared shot around the NBA.

Magic Johnson beams as he holds his new Los Angeles Lakers jersey in New York's Plaza Hotel, on June 26, 1979, shortly after being selected by the Lakers in the first round of the NBA. He is joined by NBA Commissioner Larry O'Brien (*second from right*) and his parents.

with a buzzer-beating shot, the enthusiastic rookie ran up and hugged him. Abdul-Jabbar was not amused. In a *Los Angeles Times* interview, teammate Michael Cooper recalled Abdul-Jabbar's response: "Hey, what are you doing? We've still got 81 more games to play."

In his third game, Johnson twisted his knee. Doctors feared torn ligaments, but fortunately it was only a sprain. As the season progressed, he struggled on defense, as the league's top shooting guards torched him for 30 or 40 points a game. Little by little, however, he found his groove, thanks in large part to Cooper. The young guard not only became

Johnson's good friend, but he improved Johnson's game as well. A tremendous defender, Cooper guarded Johnson in practice. Once he learned to maneuver against Coop, Johnson was able to take on anybody. Cooper also taught the rookie the secrets of good defense, such as scrutinizing game films of his opponents.

Before long, Johnson became one of the best guards in the NBA. He could score (18.0 points per game as a rookie), distribute the ball (7.3 assists per game), and rebound better than any guard in the league (7.7 rebounds per game). The Lakers boasted other standouts, as well. Abdul-Jabbar (24.8 points per game) won the NBA Most Valuable Player (MVP) Award. Jamaal "Silk" Wilkes poured in 20.0 points a game, and speedy point guard Norm Nixon put up scoring and assist numbers that were similar to Johnson's.

But Johnson was something special. His dazzling passes, enthusiastic play, and beaming smile electrified the L.A. Forum. The Lakers won 60 games in the 1979-1980 season, 13 more than the previous season and the most in the Western Conference. The Lakers also drew 582,882 fans—100,271 more than in the previous season. Johnson was so popular across the country that fans voted him a starter for the NBA All-Star Game. He was the first rookie in 11 years to be so honored.

For Johnson, Cooper told the *Los Angeles Times*, "every game was fun. And in turn, when the players are having fun, the fans are having fun. . . . It's very rare that a player can do that, to get everybody excited about playing." And he brought much more than enthusiasm to the floor. Lakers head coach Paul Westhead marveled at his toughness. "We all thought he was a movie-star player, but we found out he wears a hard hat," Westhead said, as recounted on NBA.com. "It's like finding a great orthopedic surgeon who can also operate a bulldozer."

In his very first NBA playoffs, Johnson delivered a performance for the ages. During the NBA postseason, he averaged 18.3 points, 10.5 rebounds, and 9.4 assists per game. The Lakers rolled

Los Angeles Lakers center Kareem Abdul-Jabbar (*left*) and guard
Magic Johnson (*right*) cover Philadelphia 76ers forward Caldwell
Jones in an NBA Finals game in Los Angeles, on May 4, 1980. The
pair would prove to be an unstoppable duo for the Lakers throughout their championship seasons.

over Phoenix and Seattle, winning both best-of-seven series in five games, to reach the NBA Finals against Philadelphia.

Through five games, Abdul-Jabbar dominated the court, averaging 28.5 points per game. The Lakers took a three-games-to-two lead. But when the veteran star fell to injury in the second half of Game 5, Laker fans began to panic. Who could possibly replace the mighty Abdul-Jabbar at center? Coach Westhead had the answer: his rookie guard, Magic Johnson.

Johnson jumped for the opening tipoff and played much of the game in Abdul-Jabbar's position. A guard filling in at center? "Everybody thought the guy who thought up the idea was some demented coach, the kind who reads too many books," said Westhead, as recounted in an MSN Encarta article. "But the move to center really wasn't as strange as it seemed. We knew Magic would present problems for them, and he did."

Playing not just center but all five positions, Johnson wreaked havoc from all over the court. He even employed Abdul-Jabbar's trademark shot, the "sky hook." He scored 42 points, grabbed 15 rebounds, and tallied nine assists, leading the Lakers to a 123-107 victory and the NBA championship. This was the tenth time Los Angeles had made it to the Finals but only the team's second world title. Johnson won the NBA Finals MVP Award, becoming the first rookie to do so. "You have just witnessed a miracle," Lakers owner Jerry Buss told the press after the winning game, "a magical ride by our magical man."

Abdul-Jabbar, who did not make the trip to Philadelphia, watched the game at home in California. "Big Fella, I did it for you," Johnson said to the TV cameras after the game. "I know your ankle hurts, but I want you to get up and dance."

THE DOUBLE JINX

In the span of four seasons, from 1977 through 1980, Johnson had led his teams to high school, college, and NBA championships. Abdul-Jabbar and the Philadelphia 76ers' Julius Erving may have then been the biggest superstars in the league, but Magic Johnson was clearly an exciting up-and-comer.

After the championship, Johnson again graced the cover of *Sports Illustrated*. The cover showed a smiling Earvin holding the NBA Finals MVP Award with the headline "Magic's Moment." The next season, however, Johnson again faced the double jinx—another *SI* cover and another sophomore season. And unlike his second season in college, he could not overcome the mythical hexes during his sophomore season in the NBA.

In November 1980, fate focused on Johnson's left knee. In a game against Atlanta, seven-foot-two-inch Tom Burleson banged it hard with his metal knee brace. Magic reinjured it against Dallas a few days later, then felt something snap in the knee the next night versus Kansas City. An examination revealed torn cartilage. He would have to undergo surgery and would miss several months of action.

For Johnson, rehabilitation was mental agony. He hated being away from the excitement of the game and the camaraderie of his teammates. For weeks, he spent much of his time in front of the television. In *My Life*, he recounted his TV schedule: *Ironside* started at 2:00 P.M., followed by *The Wild World of Animals*, *Barnaby Jones*, *M*A*S*H*, *Scooby Doo*, *All in the Family*, and then the 6 o'clock news. By the time of the second episode of *M*A*S*H* at 6:30, he was certifiably depressed.

At his lowest moments during rehab, Johnson wondered if he would ever be the same player again. Some players get injured and never fully recover. Maybe, after so much success so fast, his luck had ended. Fortunately, he healed well and returned to the Lakers after missing 45 games. Although his knee felt fine, he worried about reinjuring it, and for a while he lacked his former aggressiveness at game time.

Worse, a feud simmered between Johnson and fellow guard Norm Nixon. Though a friend of Johnson's, Nixon grumbled about his reduced role after Magic's return. While Nixon was a terrific point guard, he was no Johnson, who would finish

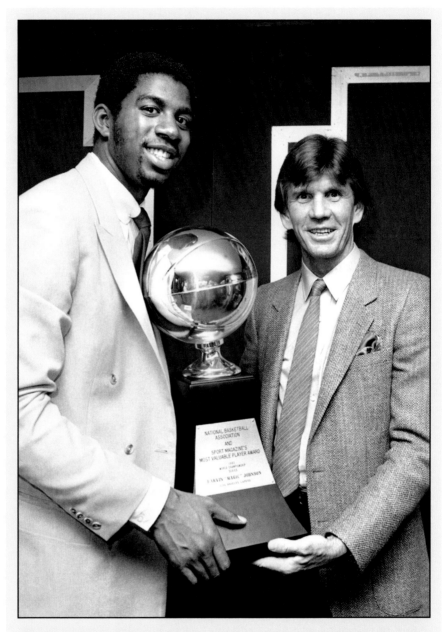

Magic Johnson (*left*) stands with Lakers coach Paul Westhead at a press conference in New York on May 22, 1980. Johnson received the Most Valuable Player Award for his part in helping the Lakers win the 1980 NBA championship series.

the season with 21.6 points, 8.6 assists, 8.6 rebounds, and an NBA-best 3.4 steals per game. Still, their subtle war of words—amplified in the newspapers—disrupted the team's chemistry.

In February 1981, Johnson became a father for the first time. It was a mixed blessing, since he was no longer in a relationship with the baby's mother, Melissa, whom he had dated during the summer of 1980 while temporarily broken up with Cookie. While Melissa raised the baby, Andre, in Lansing, Johnson made sure he was part of the boy's life. The bond between father and son grew stronger over the years.

Though the Lakers finished 54-28, they lost in the first round of the playoffs to Houston. In Game 3 of the best-of-three series, Los Angeles trailed by one with just seconds remaining. Unable to get the ball to Abdul-Jabbar, Johnson decided to take it to the basket himself. But he had no clear shot and

The Triple-Double

Magic Johnson's skill package was so unusual that the Lakers created a whole new statistic just for him. Whenever he totaled double digits in points, assists, and rebounds in a game, the team put him down for a "triple-double"—a term coined by the Lakers' public relations director, Bruce Jolesch. The term entered basketball's lexicon and eventually became an official NBA statistic.

During his NBA career, Johnson achieved 138 triple-doubles. That was far more than his next-best contemporary, Larry Bird, who amassed 59 in his career. Johnson usually scored double digits in points and tallied at least 10 assists in about half his games. So whenever he had a good rebounding night, fans got excited about a possible triple-double.

Once the stat was established, basketball gurus scoured the record books to determine who else had turned the triple trick. They found that Oscar Robertson, a do-it-all six-foot-five-inch point guard in the 1960s, had achieved 181 triple-doubles. In fact, in 1961-1962, the "Big O" *averaged* a triple-double for the season, tallying 30.8 points, 12.5 rebounds, and 11.4 assists per game. In playoff action, however, Johnson still stands wound up shooting an air ball. As he headed to Lansing for the summer, he mulled over the forgettable season.

But the drama was just beginning. During the off-season, Jerry Buss awarded Johnson the largest contract in sports history: $25 million over 25 years. Buss said he wanted Johnson around long after his playing career ended. "He may even be my coach," he said, as reported by United Press International. "Or general manager. Or maybe he'll run the team and I'll just sit back and watch. Magic is a bright kid and I plan to make him my protégé, teach him the business aspect of sports. . . . What it comes down to is that Magic is part of the family."

Johnson, who had always dreamed of being wealthy, was now set for life. But he was also worried about people's reaction. Was he basketball's equivalent of the teacher's pet? Would

out. His 30 postseason triple-doubles are nearly three times as many as anyone else has amassed.

Since the end of the Magic-Bird era, point guard Jason Kidd has been the king of the triple-double. In 2008, he recorded the one-hundredth triple-double of his career, joining Johnson and Robertson as the only members of the century club. LeBron James, a six-foot-eight-inch forward with guard skills, may one day join them.

Besides points-assists-rebounds, a player can record a triple-double with steals and blocked shots. The points-rebounds-blocks triple-double has been accomplished more than 40 times in the NBA, while the points-assists-steals trifecta had been achieved just five times up through the 2008-2009 season.

In NBA history, only four players have achieved the ultra-rare *quadruple-double*. Nate Thurmond, Hakeem Olajuwon, and David Robinson reached double digits in points, rebounds, assists, and blocks. Guard Alvin Robertson logged at least 10 points, rebounds, assists, and steals. Should a player record the unachieved quintuple-double, he will live in immortality.

his teammates and coaches resent him, and would the media and fans come down on him should he somehow falter?

Even the greatest of cynics could not have predicted what happened next. When the Lakers imploded at the start of the 1981-1982 season, Johnson was at the center of the controversy.

THE WESTHEAD INCIDENT

Back in the 1979-1980 season, Lakers head coach Jack McKinney was badly injured in a bicycle accident, and assistant Paul Westhead was promoted to his position. Westhead, who had never played in the NBA, was largely a hands-off head coach. He let the offensively potent, fast-breaking Lakers do their thing without much interference—that is, until the fall of 1981. All of a sudden, Westhead installed a rigid, slow-down offense that was predicated on feeding the ball to Kareem Abdul-Jabbar.

Most of the Lakers players thought the new offense was ridiculous. Not only was it too predictable, but it also took away their strength—running the floor. Of all the players, Johnson groused the most, especially after the team started the season with a 2-4 record. In Utah on November 18, Westhead scolded Johnson for his bad attitude during a timeout.

In the world of sports, it is a cardinal sin to criticize your teammates in front of reporters and an even worse one to disparage your coach. But when Johnson returned to the locker room, he was fuming and could not control his emotions. "I can't play here anymore," he told reporters. "I want to leave. I want to be traded."

Johnson told the reporters that he had differences with Westhead, but he did not elaborate. By the next morning, however, his "tantrum" was the talk of the L.A. sports world. Many fans condemned Johnson, claiming he had become a spoiled rich kid who thought he could always get his way. Some blamed the system: Athletes who had been handed huge contracts in recent years no longer held respect for authority figures—including their coaches.

The situation seemingly deteriorated the next day. Jerry Buss fired Westhead, replacing him with assistant coach Pat Riley. Basketball fans across America were stunned: The pampered athlete, they insisted, had got the coach fired.

In reality, Buss and Jerry West, the Lakers' general manager (and a former Lakers's superstar) had talked about replacing Westhead since the beginning of the season. They, like Johnson, did not like that he was trying to force the explosive Lakers offense into his rigid system. Buss called Johnson on the day of the firing. "Magic, I want you to stay," he told him, as Johnson recounted in *Magic*. "Jerry West, Bill Sharman, and I decided to fire Paul last Sunday and were waiting to find a replacement."

Even though Johnson had nothing to do with the firing, the myth that he had caused it persisted. Fans in visiting arenas— and even, for one game, at the L.A. Forum—showered him with boos. Over time, however, the incident was largely forgotten. Years later, Westhead spoke highly of his star player. "My three-year relationship with him wasn't even close to being a rocky one," he told a New York *Daily News* reporter.

Moreover, Johnson's evaluation of his team was right on the mark: They needed to run. New coach Pat Riley—who would become famous for his trademarked slicked-back hair, Armani suits, and immaculate tan—opened up the offense with delightful results. Under Riley, the Lakers won 50 of 71 games. They finished the season averaging 110.2 points per game, second most in the NBA. In Riley's system, Johnson flourished. He ranked second in the NBA in assists per game (9.5) and first in steals per game (2.7).

STAR POWER

It was in the 1982 playoffs that the "Showtime" Lakers emerged. The nickname "Showtime" described the team's mix of explosive offense, consistent winning, and Hollywood glitz. The last of these came in the form of celebrity fans (such as actor Jack Nicholson) and the Laker Girls (the team's dancers, including Paula Abdul of eventual *American Idol* fame). In the 1982 postseason, Los Angeles swept its first two opponents, Phoenix and San Antonio, scoring at least 110 points in each of the eight games.

In the NBA Finals, the Lakers faced Philadelphia. It looked like the 76ers would win the opener, as they led by 15 points in the third quarter. But the Lakers confounded the Sixers with a "zone trap" defense and went on a 40-11 run. Los Angeles won the game 124-117 and took the series in six games. Johnson's stat line in the finale—13 points, 13 rebounds, 13 assists—proved bad luck for the Sixers. As the buzzer sounded, the Lakers hugged one another at half-court while the ecstatic Forum crowd poured onto the floor. Johnson was named the series' MVP.

By 1982-1983, the Lakers were clearly the "class" franchise of the Western Conference, and the players became as close as family. On the court, they clicked like a finely tuned machine. Abdul-Jabbar and forward Jamaal Wilkes each averaged about 20 points per game, but Johnson made the offense tick, averaging 10.5 assists per game and leading the NBA in that category for the first of four times. He also averaged in double digits in APG for the first of nine consecutive seasons. No one had ever done that before. In fact, the previous record, held by Oscar Robinson, was just three years in a row.

Johnson racked up assists by feeding Abdul-Jabbar inside and hitting open men on the fast break, including rookie James Worthy for alley-oop jams. At six feet nine inches, he had a huge advantage at point guard. Because he stood a half-foot taller than those who guarded him, he had a clear vision of his teammates and opponents—a big deal when you have only 24 seconds to shoot. His court vision, ballhandling, instincts, and passing touch—including his signature no-look passes—made him one of the greatest floor generals in NBA history. "His playing personality is as far away from being egotistical as you can get," Abdul-Jabbar told *Sports Illustrated*. "All he wants to do is get the ball to somebody else and let them score. If you're a big man, it's not hard to like somebody like that."

The Lakers finished the season with the best record in the West (58-24), and Johnson made the All-NBA First Team for the first time. At the end of each season, sportswriters and broadcasters cast their votes for the top five players in the league—the best center, the top two forwards, and the best pair of guards. In 1983, Johnson shared things in common with the other four picks: guard Sidney Moncrief and forward Larry Bird had entered the NBA in 1979 with Johnson, and forward Julius Erving and center Moses Malone faced the Lakers in the 1983 NBA Finals.

After losing to Los Angeles in the 1982 Finals, the Sixers racked up 65 wins in the 1982-1983 season, then won eight of nine playoff games before sweeping the Lakers in the Finals. In that Finals matchup, the Lakers were shorthanded—Worthy, Nixon, and Bob McAdoo were all injured. They led all four games at the half, but the Sixers wore them down in each second half and won all four games.

Nevertheless, the undermanned Lakers had given their all, and the talented team had much to look forward to. For Magic Johnson and the Lakers, their greatest days lay ahead.

5

Battling Larry Legend

In the summer of 1986, Converse filmed a commercial in the rural town of French Lick, Indiana, home of Boston Celtics superstar Larry Bird. In the ad, Bird is shooting baskets on a remote outdoor blacktop when a black limousine glides toward him on the country road. The car's California license plate reads "LA 32." Magic Johnson rolls down the window.

"I heard Converse made a pair of Bird shoes for last year's MVP," Johnson says to his scowling rival.

"Yep," Bird replies.

"Well, they made a pair of Magic shoes for *this* year's MVP," Johnson says.

Johnson then steps out of the car and tears off his warm-up pants.

"Okay, Magic," Bird says, throwing him the ball. "Show me what you got."

The two proceed to go one-on-one.

The ad caused a buzz among basketball fans, since the Magic-Bird rivalry was the most fascinating in the NBA. While Johnson electrified arenas out West, Bird brought similar excitement to the East Coast. "Larry Legend" won NBA MVP Awards in 1984, 1985, and 1986, and Johnson took top honors in three of the next four years. Incredibly, throughout the 1980s, either Johnson's Lakers or Bird's Celtics played in the NBA Finals every single year. In three of those years, Los Angeles and Boston faced each other in the Finals—a dream matchup that shot TV ratings through the roof.

Johnson and Bird were the heart of their teams. While Johnson led the Lakers to the NBA title as a rookie in 1979-1980, Bird won the NBA Rookie of the Year Award and led Boston to 61 victories—tops in the league. They were so good, so exciting, so adored by fans that they rejuvenated the entire NBA. Interest in the league skyrocketed during the 1980s, with average NBA attendance jumping from 10,822 during the 1978-1979 season to 15,088 in 1988-1989.

Of course, other factors contributed to the league's success—the advent of cable television and a rise in people's disposable income—but it was Johnson and Bird who "elevated the league," wrote Jeff Zillgitt in *USA Today*, "electrifying the '80s with their mesmerizing brand of basketball."

A HEATED RIVALRY

The Lakers first met the Celtics in the Finals at the end of the 1983-1984 season, but with a slightly new look. Norm Nixon, the talented point guard who had been lost in Johnson's shadow, was traded to the San Diego Clippers for rookie shooting guard Byron Scott. A native of Inglewood, where the Forum was located, Scott soon became Johnson's good friend. Scott kept Johnson in stitches with his imitations of comedians Richard Pryor and Eddie Murphy. Johnson, Cooper, and Scott—known as "The Three Musketeers"—were Pat Riley's three top guards.

Kevin McHale of the Boston Celtics (*left*) and James Worthy of the
Los Angeles Lakers (*right*) struggle for a rebound as Magic Johnson
(*center*) looks on during the first game of the NBA Finals at the
Boston Garden on May 27, 1984.

With Nixon gone, Johnson had even more playmaking opportunities. During the 1983-1984 season, he averaged 13.1 assists per game, which at the time was the second-highest assist average in NBA history. On November 17 against Cleveland, he set a personal career high with 22 assists. On February 21 against Seattle, he set up 23 scores.

Although the Lakers finished the season with a modest 54-28 record, they won the Pacific Division for the third straight year and cruised through the Western Conference playoffs, winning 11 of 14 games. In a game against Phoenix, Johnson set an NBA playoff record with 24 assists. With Boston (62-20) prevailing in the Eastern Conference playoffs, the stage was set for the dream matchup: Lakers vs. Celtics, Magic vs. Bird.

The Lakers, who had lost all seven of their NBA Finals series to Boston over the years, looked to break the jinx. Coach Pat Riley also wanted to debunk the myth that his Lakers relied on talent and finesse while the Celtics were hardworking warriors. He hated that the series was billed as "Worktime vs. Showtime." Yet the Celtics were indeed a tough, physical club. Future Hall of Famers Bird, Kevin McHale, and Robert "The Chief" Parish manned the front line, along with Cedric "Cornbread" Maxwell. Gritty guards Dennis Johnson, Gerald Henderson, and Danny Ainge prepared for war in the backcourt. This series would be hotly contested, both literally and figuratively.

The Lakers survived the rugged play in Game 1, winning 115-109 in the Boston Garden. But in Game 2, Johnson and the Lakers experienced their first of several nightmarish moments. Up by two points with 15 seconds to go, Magic inbounded the ball to James Worthy, who passed crosscourt to Byron Scott. The pass never reached Scott's hands, as Henderson picked it off and drove in for a layup. Los Angeles still had a chance to win in regulation. But Dennis Johnson kept Magic from making a pass, and the buzzer sounded with the ball in his hands. The Celtics then won in overtime 124-121.

In Game 3 at the L.A. Forum, the Lakers blew the Celtics out of the gym. Magic Johnson doled out 21 assists—a record for an NBA Finals game—in a 137-104 victory. "We played like a bunch of sissies," Bird told reporters afterward, adding that he was tired of watching Johnson slap high-fives all game long.

As if to compensate for their soft play, the Celtics played a physical, mean-spirited game in the fourth battle. Not only did Bird shove Michael Cooper and mix it up with Kareem Abdul-Jabbar, but Kevin McHale deliberately knocked Kurt Rambis to the floor as the Laker forward drove for a layup. In an alarming display of bad sportsmanship, Boston's Cedric Maxwell "choked" his own neck after Worthy missed a free throw—implying that Worthy was choking under pressure.

Johnson liked to call the last couple of minutes of a close game "winning time." It was the time when the Lakers would reach deep within themselves for that something extra and take over the game. Usually it worked, but not in Game 4. Johnson's poor pass late in the game was intercepted and allowed Boston to tie the game. The Lakers still had a chance to win in regulation, but he again held the ball too long. The Celtics then won in overtime after Johnson missed two free throws. Boston fans loved to see the great superstar fail in these tight games. "Tragic Johnson," they called him.

IN HIS OWN WORDS...

In his first autobiography, *Magic* (1983), written with Richard Levin, Magic Johnson reflected on race in basketball:

> I don't know why people keep saying the NBA is in trouble because 70 percent or more of its players are black. As long as the game is played the way fans like, what difference does it make if a player is white or black? . . . When I go see a band, I don't care what color the musicians are. If it plays music I like, I'm going.

It only got worse from there. On June 8, the day of Game 5, the temperature in Boston soared to 90 degrees. The old arena, built without air conditioning, heated up like an oven, with the indoor temperature in the 90s. Players, most notably the 37-year-old Abdul-Jabbar, sucked from oxygen tanks on the sidelines. The heat did not bother Bird, however, who scored 34 points, but the Lakers fell limp, losing 121-103.

Los Angeles prevailed at home in Game 6, 119-108, but the team had to fly back to Boston for Game 7. Celtics fans were so raucous that the Lakers were given a police escort from the hotel to the Garden. Amid sauna-like conditions, the Celtics led by 14, but a late Lakers rally cut the lead to three with a minute remaining. When Maxwell knocked the ball out of Johnson's hands, the Lakers' fate was sealed. Boston won 111-102.

After the game, hundreds of ecstatic Celtics fans surrounded the Lakers' bus. Johnson and his teammates were stunned as the fans threw bottles and rocks, smashed the vehicle's windows, and rocked the bus.

Even though Johnson had totaled 95 assists in the Finals, setting a record for most assists in a playoff series, it was a horrible experience for him. "It was just heartbreaking," Johnson recalled, as reported in the *Los Angeles Times*. "We knew we were better than them, and to lose to them!"

Johnson was depressed for a long time. He went home to his apartment and did not leave it for three days. "When I called to see how he was," his mother, Christine, told *Sports Illustrated*, "he said, 'Momma, I just can't talk about it.' I guess he was just so filled with hurt."

SWEET REVENGE

Over time, the wounds began to heal—in part, perhaps, because of his luxurious new bathtub. In 1984, Johnson moved out of his apartment and into a mansion in the wealthy L.A. suburb of Bel Air. Ever since he was a child, watching his father working day and night just to pay the bills, he had dreamed of living in luxury. Of the many rooms in the house, Johnson favored the master bathroom. He could relax in the Jacuzzi and stare out the window at the canyon. "I had always dreamed of having a sunken-in tub since I saw one in a Camay soap commercial on TV," he told *Sports Illustrated*. "This girl goes through some big white pillars like she's in a castle, and then she comes walking out of this sunken-in bathtub. So sharp. When things are on my mind, I come here a lot."

Johnson also enjoyed his mansion's high-tech sound system. The former "EJ the DJ" loved listening and dancing to music—from R&B and Motown to contemporary pop and smooth jazz. He also loved going to concerts and enjoyed listening to all kinds of performers, from Madonna to David Sanborn. He even became friends with Michael Jackson.

Naturally upbeat, Johnson eventually cheered up and was raring to go for the 1984-1985 season. The Lakers were determined to reach the Finals and, they hoped, face the Celtics again. That fall, Coach Riley instructed his team to play a much more physical style of defense. Opponents took a beating on offense, then got burned by the Lakers' potent fast break. The Lakers won 62 games and led the NBA in scoring. With 18.3 points and 12.6 assists a game, Johnson made the All-NBA First Team for the third of nine consecutive seasons.

The "Fabulous" Forum became a hot spot for Hollywood celebrities. Although the price of a ticket was high, it almost always came with a victory. Johnson's "winning time" Lakers were 37-5 at home that season. Come springtime, he threw the Lakers' offense into high gear. They won each of their last six contests while averaging a scoreboard-spinning 137 points a game.

In the first round of the 1985 playoffs, Los Angeles twice topped 140 points in a three-game sweep of the Phoenix Suns. The Lakers then took 8 out of 10 against the Portland Trailblazers and Denver Nuggets. In one game against the Blazers, Johnson racked up 23 assists—one short of his own

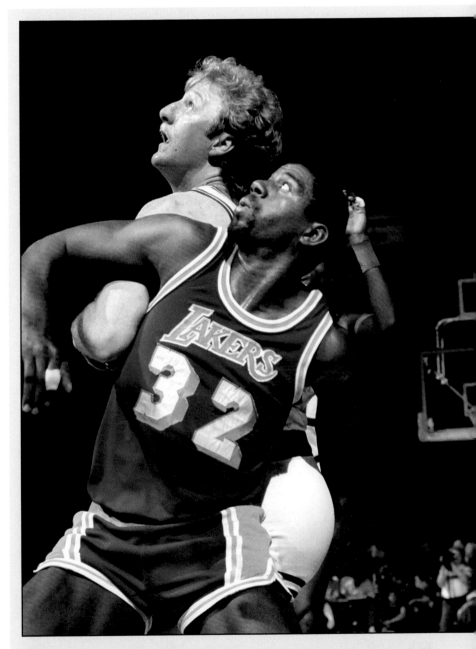

Magic Johnson of the Los Angeles Lakers and Larry Bird of the Boston Celtics battle at the Boston Garden during the second game of the 1985 NBA Finals. Their rivalry and friendship helped to define the NBA of their era.

NBA playoff record. In the NBA Finals, the Lakers again faced the Celtics, whose 63 regular-season victories gave them home-court advantage.

For the Lakers, Game 1 was another horror show. The Celtics set an NBA Finals record with 148 points while winning by 34. The press dubbed it the "Memorial Day Massacre." The Celtics outhustled the Lakers, especially Abdul-Jabbar, and Coach Riley laid into him afterward. But Johnson, forever the optimist, looked forward to the next game. "We're here

Magic Johnson's NBA Statistics

Year	Team	G	MIN	FGM	FGA	FG%	FTM	FTA
1979-1980	Lakers	77	2795	503	949	.530	374	462
1980-1981	Lakers	37	1371	312	587	.532	171	225
1981-1982	Lakers	78	2991	556	1036	.537	329	433
1982-1983	Lakers	79	2907	511	933	.548	304	380
1983-1984	Lakers	67	2567	441	780	.565	290	358
1984-1985	Lakers	77	2781	504	899	.561	391	464
1985-1986	Lakers	72	2578	483	918	.526	378	434
1986-1987	Lakers	80	2904	683	1308	.522	535	631
1987-1988	Lakers	72	2637	490	996	.492	417	489
1988-1989	Lakers	77	2886	579	1137	.509	513	563
1989-1990	Lakers	79	2937	546	1138	.480	567	637
1990-1991	Lakers	79	2933	466	976	.477	519	573
1995-1996	Lakers	32	958	137	294	.466	172	201
Totals		906	33,245	6211	11,951	.520	4960	5850

Three-point field goals: 1979-1980, 7-for-31 (.226). 1980-1981, 3-for-17 (.176). 1981-1982, 6-for-29 (.207). 1982-1983, 0-for-21. 1983-1984, 6-for-29 (.207). 1984-1985, 7-for-37 (.189). 1985-1986, 10-for-43 (.233). 1986-1987, 8-for-39 (.205). 1987-1988, 11-for-56 (.196). 1988-1989, 59-for-188 (.314). 1989-1990, 106-for-276 (.384). 1990-1991, 80-for-250 (.320). 1995-1996, 22-for-58 (.379). Totals, 325-for-1074 (.303).

because we're very good," he told reporters afterward, "so we'll throw this one out and come back Thursday." Abdul-Jabbar knew he had screwed up and came back with a vengeance in Game 2. He amassed 30 points, 17 rebounds, three blocked shots, and eight assists. The Lakers, further inspired by a Riley pep talk, won 109-102.

Back in Los Angeles, the Lakers took two of three games, with Johnson hitting three big shots in the Game 5 triumph. In Game 6 in Boston, Los Angeles expected a mighty challenge—but it

FT%	REB	AST	STL	BLK	PTS	RPG	APG	PPG
.810	596	563	187	41	1387	7.7	7.3	18.0
.760	320	317	127	27	798	8.6	8.6	21.6
.760	751	743	208	34	1447	9.6	9.5	18.6
.800	683	829 *	176	47	1326	8.6	10.5 *	16.8
.810	491	875	150	49	1178	7.3	13.1 *	17.6
.843	476	968	113	25	1406	6.2	12.6	18.3
.871	426	907 *	113	16	1354	5.9	12.6 *	18.8
.848	504	977 *	138	36	1909	6.3	12.2 *	23.9
.853	449	858	114	13	1408	6.2	11.9	19.6
.911 *	607	988	138	22	1730	7.9	12.8	22.5
.890	522	907	132	34	1765	6.6	11.5	22.3
.906	551	989	102	17	1531	7.0	12.5	19.4
.856	183	220	26	13	468	5.7	6.9	14.6
.848	6559	10,141	1724	374	17,707	7.2	11.2	19.5

Key: G (games), MIN (minutes played), FGM (field goals made), FGA (field goals attempted), FG% (field goal percentage), FTM (free throws made), FTA (free throws attempted), FT% (free throw percentage), REB (rebounds), AST (assists), STL (steals), BLK (blocks), PTS (points), RPG (rebounds per game), APG (assists per game), PPG (per game).

* = Led NBA

Source: http://www.nba.com/history/players/johnsonm_stats.html.

never came. The Lakers took a comfortable lead, quieting the crowd, and cruised to a 111-100 victory. For the first time in nine tries, the Lakers had defeated the Celtics—the league's most legendary franchise—in the NBA Finals. Both Abdul-Jabbar, who redeemed himself to win the NBA Finals MVP Award, and Johnson called it the high point of their careers. "It was a long year waiting for this moment," Johnson told the press after the game.

In *My Life*, Johnson expressed his amazement at the Boston crowd's reaction. By the end of the game, fans politely applauded the new champions—a far cry from the bus-rocking treatment of the previous year. "We had finally won their respect," he wrote, "and maybe they were embarrassed by their earlier behavior. In any case, these people knew a winner when they saw one. If somebody had to beat their Celtics, they seemed to be saying, the Lakers deserved the honor."

AMERICA'S FAVORITE PLAYER

Before the Lakers flew back home, they stopped in Washington, D.C., to meet President Ronald Reagan. At the time, reporters noted the culture clash between the Lakers of laid-back Los Angeles and the formal setting at the White House Rose Garden. Only five of the 12 Lakers wore ties to the ceremony, and Johnson was not one of them. The liberal-minded Abdul-Jabbar told the conservative president that he attended yoga classes with Reagan's son, the famously liberal Ron Reagan. Nevertheless, President Reagan, who was once the governor of California, warmly welcomed the world champions.

"I thank you all for the greeting," Reagan told the visitors,

> but I assure you the Lakers deserve the applause. . . . You showed America what pride and guts and determination, combined with talent, can do. It was Showtime yesterday at the Boston Garden as you defeated another truly great team. You knew that in Boston, it was not going to be a tea party.

Reagan even called out some of the Lakers for praise and congratulated Johnson for breaking the NBA Finals record of 60 assists in a six-game series "by an awesome 24."

After rubbing elbows with the president, the Lakers flew back to Los Angeles, where fans greeted them upon arrival. After such a bitter loss a year earlier, the summer of 1985 was a sweet one for the Magic Man. He was a three-time NBA champion and one of the biggest stars in Tinseltown. "A lot of people treat him like he's supernatural because of the way he plays," his friend Darwin Payton told *Sports Illustrated*. "I've been with him in a lot of places, and wherever he is, he's the man. When he's at a club, the stars all come over to see him."

By the mid-1980s, Johnson was clearly the most popular player in the NBA. In 1984-1985, he set a record by garnering 957,447 fan votes for the NBA All-Star Game. A year later, he became the first NBA player ever to receive a million votes. The fans voted for him not just because of his talent but because of his magnetic personality. His beaming smile lit up the arena. He doled out hugs and high-fives as often as he did assists. Fans appreciated his unselfish, winning style of basketball and idolized the man who seemingly always came through in the toughest of situations.

More than that, Johnson was kindhearted, friendly, and down-to-earth. Some athletes smiled to the TV reporters (because they were on camera) but muttered to the print journalists. Not Johnson. He respected everyone. Fans just knew that he was a genuine, first-class guy. "His appeal is universal," teammate Mitch Kupchak told *Sports Illustrated*, "and being able to communicate with everybody is a talent in itself."

Before the 1986 All-Star Game, Johnson had a sore knee, but because so many fans honored him with their votes, he played anyway, running the break with fellow Lakers James Worthy and Kareem Abdul-Jabbar. Throughout All-Star Weekend, the press buzzed about how exciting the NBA had become. Never had the All-Star Game welcomed so many superstars: Johnson, Bird, Abdul-Jabbar, Julius Erving, Moses Malone, Isiah Thomas (the

All-Star Game's MVP), Patrick Ewing, and Dominique Wilkins, to name a few. Michael Jordan, then a second-year player for the Chicago Bulls, did not play in that game due to injury.

Boston's Kevin McHale tried to explain the league's rise in popularity. "Everybody in Middle America can identify with Larry," McHale said, as reported in the *Sacramento Bee*. "The inner-city kids can identify with Isiah and Magic, and the middle-aged people can identify with Kareem!"

The Lakers enjoyed a typical season in 1985-1986. They won 62 games, 11 more than the next-best team in the West, and Johnson led the NBA with 12.6 assists per game. The Lakers swept San Antonio in the first round of the playoffs and beat Dallas in six games in the conference semifinals.

After defeating Houston in the first game of the Western Conference Finals, the Lakers expected to cruise through the series. Yet the Rockets, behind their "Twin Towers"—Hakeem Olajuwon and Ralph Sampson—won the next three games. With one second left in a tied Game 5, the seven-foot-four-inch Sampson received an inbounds pass and immediately threw it in the basket. Houston's shocking series upset prevented a third straight Lakers-Celtics Finals.

After Boston defeated Houston for the 1986 title, Larry Bird could rightfully be called the player of the 1980s (so far). Not only had he won three NBA championships and two NBA Finals MVP Awards—equaling Johnson's feats—but he had won three NBA MVP Awards. Johnson had not won any.

LAKERS VS. CELTICS, ROUND 3

It was time for Johnson to step it up, which he did in style for the 1986-1987 season. With Abdul-Jabbar approaching his fortieth birthday, Pat Riley asked Johnson to shoulder more of the scoring load. Magic was up to the task. "There's no question I felt I had to be the man this year," Johnson told the *San Diego Union*. "I wanted that burden. I wanted that pressure."

After averaging about 18 points per game for his career, Johnson averaged a career-high 23.9 PPG in 1986-1987—

including 46 against Sacramento on December 23. While upping his scoring, he never stopped dishing, leading the league with 12.2 assists per game. In one stretch late in the season, he recorded triple-doubles in four straight games. At season's end, he won his first NBA MVP Award, garnering 65 out of a possible 77 first-place votes. Michael Jordan finished second, Larry Bird third.

NBA Commissioner David Stern was proud to bestow the award on one of the NBA's good guys. "At a time when we spend so much time on allegations and other things sports are not proud of, I'm happy to come to congratulate you," he told Johnson. "I wouldn't have missed it for the world."

Johnson, meanwhile, was overcome with emotion. "This is more than I ever dreamed of," he said, as reported in the *Sun-Sentinel*. "This award I dedicate . . . to my father." Johnson undoubtedly recalled all that his father had done for him. Earvin Sr. had worked day and night, yet still had found time for his son—to play basketball with him, to attend his junior high games, to offer wise and much-needed guidance, to take him to the racetrack, just the two of them. "I'm living for him, in a sense, playing in the NBA," he continued. "I'm going to give this to him. I hope he'll be proud. I know he will."

The Lakers won 65 games in 1986-1987 and roared through the Western Conference playoffs, winning 11 of 12 games. Once again, they faced Larry Bird and the Celtics in the NBA Finals. Boston had won the first matchup in 1984. The Lakers then prevailed in the next battle in 1985. Who would emerge victorious in the next round?

Johnson had carried the team all year and did not let up in the Finals. In Game 1, he led the Lakers to victory with 29 points, 13 assists, eight rebounds, and—remarkably—zero turnovers. His 20 assists in Game 2 led to another victory. And although Boston won on its home floor in Game 3, Johnson hit the winning shot in a Game 4 thriller. (The Celtics led 106-105 until Johnson buried a 10-foot running hook shot with two seconds left.) "You're probably going to get beat [by the Lakers] on a sky hook," said Bird after the game, referring to Abdul-Jabbar's patented shot, "but you don't expect it from Magic."

Boston won Game 5, but the Lakers breezed past the Celtics in Game 6, winning 106-93, thanks in part to Johnson's 19 assists. Johnson did it all in the Finals, even at the free-throw line, where he sank 24 of 25. Following the Lakers' victory, he became only the fifth player in NBA history to win the NBA MVP Award and the Finals MVP Award in the same season. "He's the best," Riley proclaimed to the press afterward. "I think his performance in the regular season and the playoffs proves that. We wouldn't be anywhere without him."

Although Johnson had beaten Bird two titles to one, he did not let the success go to his head. In the summer of 1986, while filming the Converse commercial, the two rivals became good friends and have remained so ever since.

In April 2009, the old rivals got together to commemorate the thirtieth anniversary of their famous Michigan State-Indiana State championship game. Sitting alongside Bird, Johnson explained to reporters why basketball fans were fascinated with the two of them. "We played the game the right way," he said.

> We didn't play it for ourselves; we played it for our team. We were two unique guys being over six foot eight, being able to handle the ball, being able to score inside or outside, being able to make the right pass to our teammates. Because we really didn't care about scoring. We really cared about win-ning the game.
>
> And then you have one player black, one player white. One player who smiles, one who don't.

Johnson turned to Bird and saw that his friend was actually grinning. "Except right now," Johnson laughed, putting his hand on Bird's shoulder. "I think it was just special."

6

The Remaining Glory

On August 2, 1987, Magic Johnson hosted a benefit basketball game for the United Negro College Fund. He called it "A Midsummer Night's Magic," and, not surprisingly, all the stars showed up. Johnson had first staged the event in 1986 at UCLA's Pauley Pavilion. It was such a success that the 1987 version was held at the larger L.A. Forum. With a star-studded cast of players, including Magic himself, they sold out the arena. The game raised more than a half-million dollars for charity.

Such NBA stars as Isiah Thomas, Alex English, Dominique Wilkins, "Sir" Charles Barkley, Hakeem "The Dream" Olajuwon, and Clyde "The Glide" Drexler played in the extravaganza. Defense was, shall we say, discouraged, to the delight of the fans. In the end, Johnson's white team lost to the blue team after buddy Thomas hit two free throws with one second left. Final score: 180-178.

Johnson dazzled all night long. His fast-break passes to Charles Barkley resulted in thunderous dunks. On one play, he uncorked a no-look, behind-the-back pass to good friend Michael Cooper, who swished a three-pointer. At halftime, "EJ the DJ" emceed a three-point contest, which featured pal Byron Scott. Johnson was overjoyed by the whole experience. "Any time you can get those guys in the same game and put on a show like that," he told reporters afterward, "anybody in their right mind would be happy and excited. And I'm happy and excited."

Johnson enjoyed vacationing and luxuriating as much as anyone, but more than anything else, he loved helping others. In the summer of 1987, he held a 4-H rally for 3,500 youngsters in East Lansing, Michigan, and staged basketball camps in Michigan and California. At the camps, he often had to curb his enthusiasm. "One important thing is I try to be stern right away, teach them discipline, tell them that if they're here just to be with Magic Johnson, they should pack up and leave," he told a reporter for the *San Diego Union.* "I'm here to teach them basketball, and once we get that established, it's all right. . . . If I come in laughing and joking, then all they do is laugh and joke all week."

TEACHING THE BAD BOYS A LESSON

Similarly, Lakers coach Pat Riley was all business during training camp for the 1987-1988 season. Riley was always guarding against complacency. If he thought his players were giving less than a 100-percent effort, he let them have it.

With Kareem Abdul-Jabbar no longer a major force on the court, the Lakers relied heavily on their perimeter players. James Worthy, Scott, and Johnson all averaged about 20 points per game in 1987-1988. Behind Johnson's supreme leadership, the Lakers enjoyed another great season, winning 62 games and their seventh straight Pacific Division crown. Although Chicago's Michael Jordan emerged as the NBA's premier player—winning his first NBA MVP Award that season— Johnson finished third in the balloting. (As evidence of his dominance throughout his career, he never finished lower than third in MVP voting from 1982-1983 through 1990-1991.)

The Lakers swept San Antonio in the first round of the play-offs, but they needed seven games to defeat both the Utah Jazz and Dallas Mavericks. Johnson prepared for battle against the Detroit Pistons, who made the NBA Finals for the first time in franchise history.

In every previous season, Johnson played only one game a year in his home state of Michigan, and his family would bring a home-cooked meal to feed the team. But in June 1988, he would face the Pistons seven games in a row. During the series, Johnson did not want to visit his family, knowing he would be tense and short-tempered. Like most NBA players of the era, he hated playing the Pistons. The "Bad Boys" were not only one of the toughest defensive teams in NBA history, but they played a rough and often dirty brand of basketball.

The Pistons were loaded with fascinating characters, including point guard Isiah Thomas, an articulate man with an angelic smile who played with the heart of a lion. He was one of Johnson's best pals. Joe Dumars was such a gentleman that the NBA would one day name its good-sportsmanship trophy after him. The tall, lanky John "Spider" Salley did stand-up comedy in his spare time. Dennis Rodman was on his way to becoming the league rebel, with tattoos, body piercings, and colorful hair dyes.

DID YOU KNOW?

Magic Johnson and Detroit Pistons superstar Isiah Thomas were such good friends that Johnson had an "Isiah Thomas Room" in his home. Throughout the 1980s, they were the two best point guards in the NBA.

Big men Rick Mahorn and Bill Laimbeer were the nastiest of Detroit's Bad Boys. They made their living throwing elbows and shoving players in the lane. Laimbeer may be one of the most despised players in NBA history. He frequently whined to officials about calls and often performed the "Laimbeer flop"—feigning he was fouled by falling to the floor.

If that was not enough, Pat Riley added to the pressure by guaranteeing that the Lakers would repeat as champions in 1988. In Game 1 of the Finals, after Johnson and Thomas kissed each other on the cheek before the tipoff, the fired-up Pistons crushed the Lakers at the Forum. Then Johnson caught the flu, forcing him to miss the next day's practice.

Although still sick in Games 2 and 3, Johnson managed to lead the Lakers to two victories. Game 4 was another story. Thomas shoved his pal Johnson on one play and whacked Magic in the jaw with his forearm later on. The Bad Boys evened the series with an 111-86 rout. The Lakers, however, played exceedingly rough in Game 5 in Detroit, only to get into foul trouble and lose the game. To win the series, they needed to take the remaining two games, both on their home turf in Los Angeles.

Game 6 was an all-out war. Thomas scored 25 points in the third quarter despite playing on a badly swollen ankle. The Lakers trailed 102-101 with 14 seconds left when Laimbeer "fouled" Abdul-Jabbar during Kareem's missed sky hook. Replays failed to prove that a foul had been committed, but Abdul-Jabbar went to the line and sank both free throws to win the game.

In Game 7, the Lakers led by 15 points, but then the Pistons roared back. A 28-foot three-pointer by Laimbeer closed the gap to 106-105 with six seconds to go. Johnson followed with a quick, long pass to A.C. Green for a layup, but Thomas had a last chance for a tying three-pointer. Yet before the buzzer sounded, fans stormed the floor and Thomas collided with Johnson. No call was made, and the Lakers had won their

Although both had pushed and shoved each other during competition, Isiah Thomas of the Detroit Pistons (*right*) and Magic Johnson of the Los Angeles Lakers (*left*) said they still love each other, despite doing what they have to do on the basketball court. Here, the two kiss each other on the cheek on June 16, 1988, before the jump ball.

fifth title of the decade. Johnson had played extremely well throughout the playoffs, becoming the first NBA player ever to top 300 assists in one postseason (303). Nevertheless, "Big Game" James Worthy won the NBA Finals MVP Award.

"I don't know what I have left—I'm just glad it's over," Johnson told reporters afterward.

The Honor Roll

Below are some of Magic Johnson's greatest achievements in the NBA:

- Won NBA championships with the Los Angeles Lakers in 1980, 1982, 1985, 1987, and 1988.
- Won the NBA Finals MVP Award in 1980, 1982, and 1987.
- Earned the NBA MVP Award in 1986-1987, 1988-1989, and 1989-1990.
- Ranked in the top three in NBA MVP balloting every year from 1982-1983 through 1990-1991.
- Made the All-NBA First Team each season from 1982-1983 through 1990-1991.
- Played in 12 NBA All-Star Games.
- Named MVP of the NBA All-Star Game in 1990 and 1992.
- Set the NBA record for career assists in regular-season play with 10,141 (since broken).
- Holds the NBA record for assists per game in regular-season play (11.2).
- Holds NBA postseason records for career assists (2,346) and career assists per game (12.3).
- Won an Olympic gold medal in 1992.
- Won the NBA's J. Walter Kennedy Citizenship Award in 1992.
- Elected to the Naismith Memorial Basketball Hall of Fame in 2002.

This has been the toughest championship series I've ever been in, and it's not just because of the three seven-game series. Playing against Isiah in the championship was so hard for me. I tried to stay away from him and tried not to be his friend. . . . It's the most difficult thing I've ever had to do.

AIMING FOR A THREE-PEAT

One thing was sure: Johnson was not going to follow his coach and guarantee another NBA championship. "I guarantee . . . that I'm going to have a good summer," he told the press after the final NBA Finals game. "And that's all I'm going to guarantee."

Although no Laker predicted a third straight title, behind the scenes, the team did have a new goal: a "three-peat." Nowadays, that term is used in sports all the time, but it was the Lakers who made it popular. Byron Scott uttered the term after the 1988 championship, and Coach Riley registered a trademark for the term. If the Lakers did three-peat, those who manufactured T-shirts and caps with "three-peat" on them would have to pay Riley money.

From October 1988 through early June 1989, the Lakers seemed primed to three-peat. The team won a division-best 57 games and still maintained the highest-scoring offense in the league. Power forward A.C. Green racked up rebounds, and Johnson had one of his best seasons, tallying 22.5 points, 12.8 assists, and 7.8 rebounds per game. Johnson, who had developed into a very good free-throw shooter in the mid- to late 1980s, was nearly automatic in 1988-1989. He made 91.1 percent of his shots at the line, the best mark in the NBA.

In a two-man race for the NBA MVP Award, Johnson beat out Michael Jordan. Riley opined why his MJ won the award over the other MJ, who had averaged a league-best 32.5 points per game. "[He's] a leader, a motivator, a player-coach on the floor," Riley said, as reported by the Associated Press. Added Worthy in the same AP story: "It's the extras, his approach and attitude, the unseen things that make the difference with Earvin."

Those "extras" helped the Lakers zoom through the Western Conference playoffs in 1989. The team swept Portland, then Seattle, then Phoenix—11 wins in a row. The Lakers were well rested and confident entering their rematch against the Pistons in the NBA Finals. But then disaster struck.

Byron Scott tore a hamstring before Game 1, and the Lakers lost 109-97. Then in the third quarter of Game 2, Johnson tore *his* hamstring. As Johnson lay in pain, his teammates looked at him with doom in their eyes. Without their two star guards, including their peerless leader, they had little chance of winning the series.

Led by Worthy, the Lakers battled heroically. They lost Game 2 and Game 3 (in which Johnson played just five minutes) by just three points each. Detroit finished off the sweep at the Forum with a score of 105-97. With 47 seconds left in the finale, Kareem Abdul-Jabbar left the game amid thunderous applause. The 42-year-old center was about to retire after 20 legendary seasons in the NBA. His career total of 38,387 regular-season points was—and remains—an NBA record.

Throughout the 1989-1990 season, the Lakers continued to dominate, winning a league-best 63 games. Johnson, who averaged 22.3 points per game, repeated as the league's Most Valuable Player. He also won the All-Star Game MVP Award after scoring a game-high 22 points—including four of six from the three-point line. Moreover, he became a three-point threat for the first time that season, swishing 106 triple tries at an excellent 38.4-percent rate.

Still, the Lakers knew that the playoff competition would be harder than ever, as five Western Conference teams had won at least 54 games in 1989-1990. One of them was the Phoenix Suns, who delighted in a five-game triumph over the Lakers in the conference semifinals. After this disappointing season, Pat Riley resigned as coach.

Some hoops historians consider that series the end of the Lakers' dynasty—and if it was, what a run it had been. Over an 11-year stretch, they had won 10 Pacific Division titles, had reached the NBA Finals eight times, and had won five NBA championships. Few pro teams in American sports history have been so good for so long. And who was the man running the show each and every year? Magic Johnson.

MAGIC INC.

In the fall of 1990, *Sports Illustrated* revealed another side of the Lakers superstar. Johnson appeared on the cover in a suit and smoking an expensive cigar next to the headline "Magic Inc." Johnson, the cover story revealed, had become a successful businessman and a generous philanthropist. In addition to his Lakers salary ($2.4 million in 1990-1991), he was making at least $9 million a year in business ventures. Among other things, he had founded a sports apparel company and was the general partner of a soft-drink distributorship. The article caught a lot of fans by surprise. "People may know Magic," he said in the *SI* piece, "but they don't know Earvin."

Johnson said that he wanted to amass between $100 million to $200 million so that he could buy a sports team. "And it doesn't have to be the Lakers," he told *SI*, "it doesn't even have to be an NBA team. I'm a sports fan. If baseball became available before basketball, I'd be right there. I want to do big business."

Although ambitious, Johnson was not greedy. In fact, he was extremely generous with his money. The article reported that Johnson had raised or given more than $2 million to charities in 1990 alone, including $1.5 million to the United Negro College Fund, $300,000 to the Muscular Dystrophy Association, and $300,000 to the City of Hope, an institution that strives to find cures for life-threatening diseases.

Though he was preparing for a career in business, Johnson—at age 31—could still hoop it up. Back on the court for the 1990-1991 season, he averaged 19.4 points and 12.5 assists per

March 16, 1992.

Pay to the order of **MAGIC JOHNSON FOUNDATION, INC.,** $ **25,000**

Twenty-five Thousand and no/xx _____ Dollars.

Neil Diamond

Magic Johnson is almost as well known for his charity work and sound business sense as he is for being one of the all-time pro basketball greats. Here, Johnson accepts for his foundation a donation from entertainer Neil Diamond on March 16, 1992.

game while shooting 90.6 percent at the free-throw line. And on April 15, 1991, he recorded his 9,888th career assist, breaking Oscar Robertson's NBA record.

To commemorate Johnson's achievement, the Lakers-Mavericks game was stopped and Lakers fans honored him with a standing ovation. Johnson thanked his current and former teammates, owner Jerry Buss, and his mom and dad, who were watching on television. "Without those two beautiful people, the 'Magic Makers,' I wouldn't be here," an emotional Johnson told the crowd. "I know my dad is at home sitting in the same seat that he used to sit in and teach me how to play the game. Mom and Dad, thank you. I love you so much."

Earlier that day, Robertson sent Johnson a telegram. "Magic Man, congratulations on your new success," he wrote.

"You have been a tremendous asset, statesman, humanitarian, etc., to the Lakers, to the NBA, and the USA with your years of true consistent basketball. You having the assist record will only add to its prestige."

Under new coach Mike Dunleavy in 1990-1991, the Lakers dropped to second in the Pacific Division with 58 wins. However, they went 11-3 in the Western Conference playoffs en route to a matchup with Michael Jordan's Chicago Bulls in the NBA Finals.

TRANSITIONS

After being ousted from the playoffs for three straight years by the Bad Boy Pistons, the Bulls got back at their hated rivals in 1991. They swept Detroit in the Eastern Conference Finals and entered the NBA Finals as a team on a mission. After Los Angeles stole the opener at Chicago Stadium 93-91, Jordan led the Bulls to four straight victories over a Lakers team that was battling injuries. For the series, Jordan averaged 31.2 points and 11.4 assists per game.

"He was MVP during the year and MVP during the play-offs, [and] as an individual he's unbelievable," Johnson said, as reported by the Associated Press. Clearly, the torch had been passed. While the 1980s had belonged to Magic Johnson, Jordan would become the player who owned the 1990s, leading the Bulls to six NBA titles in the decade and outdoing Magic's 1980s total by one.

In many ways, Johnson was entering new stages in his life. On September 14, 1991, he married Cookie Kelly. The couple had been through an on-again, off-again relationship since college. In 1985, Johnson had broken their engagement, claiming that the demands of marriage would infringe on his basketball obligations. But on his wedding day, "I knew . . . that I had made the right choice," he wrote in *My Life*. "To see her walking down the aisle with her father, looking so beautiful in that dress—it was just breathtaking. It was the happiest day of my life, and the best thing that had ever happened to me."

But just six weeks after this very happy occasion, Johnson received the worst news of his life. On October 25, after checking in to his hotel in Utah for a preseason game, Magic got a phone call. It was Dr. Michael Mellman, the Lakers' team physician. "Earvin," he said, as recounted in *My Life*. "I'd like you to fly back here and see me right away."

"Why?" Johnson asked.

"I've just learned that you failed your insurance physical."

The doctor did not explain the reason, preferring to tell Johnson in person. He took the next plane back to Los Angeles, wondering what was wrong with him.

7

Down . . . But Not Out

The waiting room was empty when Magic Johnson and his agent, Lon Rosen, arrived to see Dr. Michael Mellman on October 25, 1991. When Mellman called them into his office, Johnson noticed the physician's pale face and troubled expression and prepared for the worst.

The doctor told Johnson that during his life-insurance physical exam, he had tested positive for HIV, the virus that causes AIDS. Johnson was in shock. He did not cry, shout, or challenge the results. He just sat there in a daze.

Like many Americans, Johnson had only a vague understanding of the virus and the disease. He knew that AIDS had been a growing epidemic in the United States since the early 1980s and that AIDS patients seemed to wither away and die within a few years of contracting the disease.

Mellman also explained that Johnson had HIV, not AIDS. And although HIV leads to AIDS, many people had lived up to 10 years with HIV before developing AIDS symptoms. In 10 years, Johnson would be just 42 years old.

Johnson also wondered how he had contracted the virus. He knew that it was often a sexually transmitted disease, but he had assumed that it was confined to drug users and those in the lesbian, gay, and transgender community. That assumption was wrong. Johnson was heterosexual and drug-free. He would later indicate that he contracted the virus through sexual intercourse with a woman he had been involved with before he resumed his relationship with Cookie.

Johnson worried about Cookie. Could he have passed HIV on to her? Another horrible thought: Cookie had recently discovered that she was pregnant. Was the baby infected as well? The doctor said he would give Cookie a blood test in two days, on Sunday morning, and it would take several more days before they would know if she was infected.

That evening at home, Johnson broke the news to Cookie. When he gave her the option to walk away from their marriage, she reportedly slapped him in the face. The offer had insulted her. She was not a coward; she loved him and would stand by her husband.

After Cookie's blood test on Sunday, the couple waited until Thursday, Halloween, to hear the results. Cookie had tested negative, meaning she and the unborn baby were fine. Meanwhile, Johnson had to wait until Wednesday, November 6, to talk to Dr. David Ho, an expert on HIV and AIDS. Ho would analyze Johnson's test results and give him the results then.

In the meantime, Johnson kept his disease a secret. He told only selected family members and friends, including Lakers owner Jerry Buss. The Lakers told the media that Johnson had the flu and would be taking time off to fully recover. As the days passed, reporters and fans wondered why it was taking him so long to get over the flu.

On Wednesday, Dr. Ho told Johnson that the virus had yet to have much of an effect on his immune system. But continuing

Magic Johnson and his bride, Cookie, exit the church on September 14, 1991, following their wedding ceremony in Johnson's hometown of Lansing, Michigan. Just weeks after this happy occasion, the Johnsons would learn that Magic had tested positive for HIV.

to play basketball, he said, would put too much stress on his body. He strongly recommended that Johnson retire, and Magic concurred. He would hold a press conference at the Forum on Friday to announce that he had HIV and was leaving the game he loved.

On Thursday morning, however, a rumor spread in the media that Johnson had AIDS. Johnson, Rosen, and the Lakers responded by moving up the press conference to 3:00 P.M. on Thursday. Johnson and Rosen called friends and family ahead of time to break the news. Johnson asked his father to tell his son, Andre, what was going on; Magic would talk to him personally later on. Rosen called Pat Riley, Kareem Abdul-Jabbar,

Larry Bird, Isiah Thomas, Michael Jordan, and others. All were shocked—Jordan broke into tears—but they all expressed their support for him.

Before the press conference, Johnson broke the news to his teammates. They cried and embraced him, and he too broke down in tears. Then it was time to talk to the world.

"PRAY FOR EARVIN"

Cookie accompanied Johnson to the press conference. So did Rosen, Dr. Mellman, Abdul-Jabbar, and the Lakers' general manager, Jerry West. An army of reporters and camera crews, too many to fit in the large room, attended the anticipated and dreaded event. National television networks broadcast the event live, and CNN beamed the event across the globe.

Johnson cut right to the chase in his opening remark. "Because of the HIV virus that I have attained," he said,

> I will have to retire from the Lakers today. I do not have the AIDS disease. I plan on going on living for a long time, bugging you guys like I always have, so you'll see me around. I plan on being with the Lakers and the league for a while and going on with my life.

Later in the conference, Johnson was already sounding like a spokesman for HIV/AIDS awareness. "I want young people to realize they can practice safe sex," he said. "I think people can be a little naive about this issue. They think it can never happen to you; it can only happen to other people. They think only gay people can get it or whatever. Well, I'm here to say it can happen to anybody, even me, Magic Johnson."

Johnson's announcement drew major news coverage for days. Millions of sports fans, who had been inspired by Johnson's exuberance and winning-time smile, were socked with sober reality: Even the mightiest champions can fall. Life is short. We are all vulnerable. Mostly, people just felt sad for Magic Johnson.

That evening, Pat Riley, who after leaving the Lakers had become coach of the New York Knicks, led a moment of silence for Johnson. He told the crowd at New York's Madison Square Garden: "In your own voice, in your own beliefs, in your own way, pray for Earvin and the one million people afflicted with an insidious disease who need our understanding." He then recited the Lord's Prayer.

In the hours and days after the press conference, Johnson's friends expressed their feelings. "The thought that he will not put on No. 32 again is gut-wrenching," said Lakers radio broadcaster Chick Hearn, as reported by the Associated Press. "He is a goodwill ambassador for basketball. I don't know if basketball will ever recover from this."

"This man did not touch an entire city; he touched the whole world," said Knicks guard Mark Jackson, as reported in the *Seattle Times*. George Fox, Magic's high school coach, told the Associated Press: "It's unreal what happened. He was a dream come true, a product of Lansing, just a beautiful person that bettered everyone that came in contact with him. Anybody that knew him has got to be devastated."

EDUCATING ABOUT HIV/AIDS
Not everyone, however, showed sympathy for Johnson. Since AIDS had emerged in the 1980s, doctors, educators, and public-service ads had expressed the best way to contain the disease: safe sex (meaning the use of condoms) and abstaining from sex. Johnson, like many other star athletes, had had sex with many women. Since he had contracted HIV, people concluded that he had not always practiced safe sex. "Johnson has not been a hero to women," wrote Sally Jenkins in *Sports Illustrated*. "He has been a hazard. If indeed he was infected with HIV through heterosexual contact, he has been their

Magic Johnson meets with President George H.W. Bush in the Oval Office of the White House in Washington, D.C., on January 15, 1992. Johnson, the newest member of the National Commission on AIDS, said the president needed to "speak out more" on AIDS and spend more federal money to fight the deadly disease.

victim and, potentially, their victimizer." Jenkins meant that if Johnson had contracted HIV from one woman and then had unprotected sex with women afterward, he was putting all of the other women's lives in danger.

Then again, Johnson was courageous enough to publicly admit that he had HIV. He did not have to give anyone a reason for his retirement. Moreover, as one of the most famous people ever to make the disclosure, he became a godsend for HIV/AIDS awareness. Referring to Johnson's announcement, Fred Allemann of the Cascade AIDS Project said, as reported in the *Seattle Post-Intelligencer*: "He probably saved thousands of lives just in that one act." Heterosexuals in particular were scared. Upon hearing the news, New York Giants superstar linebacker Lawrence Taylor said, as reported in the *Houston Chronicle*, "I'm going to get my test done tomorrow."

One day after his press conference, Johnson began his crusade to fight HIV/AIDS. He appeared on his friend Arsenio Hall's late-night talk show, where he talked about confronting AIDS head-on. "We don't have to run from it," he said. "We don't have to be ashamed of it. You don't have to run from me like 'Oh-oh, here comes Magic.'" He said that one myth that he wanted to explode was that "it can only happen to gay people. That's so wrong. I was naive."

On November 13, 1991, President George H.W. Bush wrote a letter to Johnson, asking him to join the 12-member National Commission on AIDS. Although Johnson graciously accepted, when he learned that the federal government had not done enough to battle AIDS, which by that point had killed more than 70,000 Americans, he decided to take a bold stance.

In January 1992, he met with President Bush at the White House and handed him a letter that he and AIDS activist Elizabeth Glaser had written. In it, they urged him to make the fight against AIDS a high priority and indicated how much money they thought was needed to properly fund research and treatment. (The president had rarely mentioned AIDS in his public addresses, and Congress had appropriated little funding for AIDS research and for treatment of AIDS patients.) Before and after his meeting with the president, Johnson talked frankly to reporters. "He [Bush] needs to do a lot," he said. "He hasn't done a lot. He's going to have to allocate some money and get more involved."

AIDS activists understood how important Johnson was to their cause. Janice Jireau, a 41-year-old woman who was HIV-positive, told him that day, as reported by the *Chicago Tribune*: "We don't have a voice, Magic. We don't have anybody to stand up for us. . . . We need you. We're suffering; we need your help."

TEARS OF PAIN AND JOY

And Johnson did help, especially with young people. In 1992, *A Conversation with Magic Johnson* aired on Nickelodeon and public television. Sharing the set with children ages 8 to 14, Johnson and show host Linda Ellerbee talked frankly about sex and HIV. Ellerbee showed a condom and explained how it is used. He said that the "safest sex is no sex" and urged compassion for those with HIV and AIDS.

The most poignant moment in the show was when an HIV-positive girl, about eight years old, broke into tears. "I want

Basic Facts About HIV and AIDS

- The acronym HIV stands for human immunodeficiency virus, which causes acquired immunodeficiency syndrome (AIDS).

- When HIV enters the body, it lives and multiplies within white blood cells. HIV weakens the white blood cells, whose purpose is to protect the body from disease.

- A person with AIDS has a weakened immune system and cannot fight off certain illnesses and infections.

- A person with HIV carries the virus in certain body fluids, including blood, semen, breast milk, and vaginal secretions. The virus can be transmitted only if these HIV-infected fluids enter the bloodstream of another person.

- An HIV-infected person can transmit the virus to another person through unprotected sexual intercourse (without a latex condom).

- Worldwide, some 40 million people are afflicted with HIV.

- More than 25 million people have died of AIDS since 1981.

- It is believed that more than one million Americans are living with HIV or AIDS.

- It is estimated that about one-half of those Americans who have HIV do not know it because they have not had themselves tested.

people to know . . . that we're just normal people," she said. Johnson reached over to comfort her. "You don't have to cry," he told her. "Because we are normal people, okay? We are. It's okay to cry."

In the spring of 1992, Johnson published a book, *What You Can Do to Avoid AIDS*, aimed at teenagers. The book frankly explains vitally important issues, such as precisely how HIV is transmitted. One of the book's important messages is that it is extremely unlikely, if not impossible, to get AIDS through casual contact with another person.

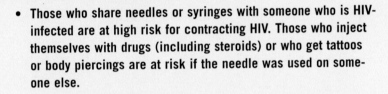

- Those who share needles or syringes with someone who is HIV-infected are at high risk for contracting HIV. Those who inject themselves with drugs (including steroids) or who get tattoos or body piercings are at risk if the needle was used on someone else.

- An HIV-infected person cannot infect another person through casual contact, such as hand-holding or hugging. It is possible but extremely unlikely to pass the virus through kissing. HIV cannot be passed through breath, tears, sweat, urine, or insect bites.

- Mother-to-fetus HIV transmission has dropped dramatically in the United States because pregnant women are tested for HIV and medications can prevent the transmission of HIV to the child.

- In the United States, screening the blood supply for HIV has virtually eliminated the risk of infection through blood transfusions.

- Advancements in drug therapy have helped people with HIV and AIDS live longer, healthier lives. (Many people can now live more than 20 years with HIV before developing symptoms of AIDS.) However, there is still no vaccine, or cure, for HIV or AIDS.

Johnson also established the Magic Johnson Foundation, which flourishes to this day. The foundation's goals are wide in scope. Over the years, the foundation's "I Stand with Magic" program has provided free HIV/AIDS tests to some 40,000 Americans. Moreover, the program has educated hundreds of thousands of people about HIV. Its organizers, according to the official Web site, work "to develop programs and support community-based organizations that address the educational, health and social needs of ethnically diverse, urban communities." Specifically, the foundation has provided college scholarships to more than 800 minority high school students. It holds an annual Children's Mardi Gras and holiday toy drive and has opened 20 Magic Johnson Community Empowerment Centers in underserved communities.

In 2005, a new Community Empowerment Center opened in Eastover, South Carolina. Only 800 people lived in the small, impoverished, African-American community. Nevertheless, nearly 1,000 people showed up to see Johnson at the center's grand opening. Johnson nearly cried because the area reminded him so much of his childhood neighborhood in Lansing. The Eastover center received 25 computers, offered adult training for new nurses and truck drivers, and provided

IN HIS OWN WORDS...

In February 1992, shortly after he began his HIV/AIDS work, Magic Johnson said:

The message first is that people with the [HIV] virus can live on, lead productive lives and run, jump, whatever. It's not just people with the virus. It's handicapped people, people who've had stuff happen to them. You can continue to live. Life doesn't stop.

Source: *Daily News of Los Angeles*, February 10, 1992.

free golf and tennis lessons. Classes for children emphasized science, math, and character development.

In September 1992, Johnson resigned from the National Commission on AIDS. In a letter to President Bush, he said the commission and the president were not doing enough to fight the epidemic.

Though Johnson retired from the NBA in 1991, he enjoyed some exhilarating moments on the basketball court in 1992. First came his joyous, emotional appearance at the 1992 NBA All-Star Game. A week later, the Lakers retired his number 32 in a teary-eyed ceremony at the Forum, where he was showered with gifts. NBA players made a $600,000 donation to the Magic Johnson Foundation. And Larry Bird gave him a piece of the Boston Garden's fabled parquet floor.

Johnson had many people to thank that day, particularly his parents. He said of his father:

> Without you sitting there, every Sunday, sitting by me and pointing out different things about basketball . . . getting me on that truck every day in the morning, making me go to work with you . . . I wouldn't have known what hard work is all about. I love you so much.

"And Mom," he added, "if you took a picture of you and took a picture of me, it's like the same person because I stole everything you got. And the thing I tried to take the most was your heart, because you're so beautiful. And you know I love you always."

BACK IN THE GAME

Throughout 1992, Johnson expressed the possibility that he might return to the NBA. By taking good care of himself and through proper medication, he was feeling great. One thing was for sure, he was going to play in the 1992 Summer Olympics in Barcelona, Spain.

That year, for the first time in history, professional athletes were allowed to compete in the Olympic games. That meant that U.S. head basketball coach Chuck Daly could stock his roster with NBA superstars. All the greats agreed to be part of the so-called "Dream Team." Joining Magic Johnson were Michael Jordan, Larry Bird, Charles Barkley, David Robinson, Patrick Ewing, Karl Malone, Scottie Pippen, Chris Mullin, Clyde Drexler, John Stockton, and one college player: future NBA All-Star Christian Laettner. "It was like Elvis and the Beatles put together," Daly said, as recalled by NBA.com. "Traveling with the Dream Team was like traveling with 12 rock stars."

During the Olympics' opening ceremonies, athletes from other countries acted like Johnson's groupies. Johnson told *Sports Illustrated*:

> Marching in the opening ceremonies was one of the wildest, most incredible things that ever happened to me. Everybody running over, breaking lines to get an autograph, a picture or to just shake my hand—I never thought that would happen. Never. We're used to attention, but I just couldn't believe that that many athletes from that many countries would want to meet me.

The Dream Team won all eight of its games, including a 116-48 clock-cleaning of Angola. USA's 32-point victory over Croatia in the gold-medal game was the closest contest. Opposing teams were just thrilled to be on the same court with the global superstars. One opponent waved to his teammate on the bench, urging him to take a picture of him guarding Johnson.

Throughout the games, everybody asked Johnson to flash his world-famous smile. "Everybody," Johnson told *SI*. "I'll hear that in my sleep. 'Ma-jeek! Ma-jeek! Please smile for me. Smile for the camera.' And as you know, I've always been able to smile."

Magic Johnson, playing for the U.S. Olympic team, guards against Toni Kukoc of Croatia, in the men's final at the Summer Olympics in Barcelona, Spain, on August 8, 1992. The United States defeated Croatia 117-85 to win the gold medal. It was the first time in Olympic history that professional players from the NBA were allowed to participate.

Johnson played limited minutes in the Olympics. But he felt so good and missed basketball so much, that in September he announced he was returning to the Lakers. However, a few NBA players began to voice their opposition, just as they had before the 1992 All-Star Game. Utah

Jazz superstar Karl Malone feared that the virus could pass through open wounds. "Look at this, scabs and cuts all over me," he remarked to the *New York Times*. "I get these every night, every game. They can't tell you that you're not at risk, and you can't tell me there's one guy in the NBA who hasn't thought about it."

"Everybody's talking about it," the Cleveland Cavaliers' Gerald Wilkins told the *New York Times*. "Some people are scared. This could be dangerous to us all, but you're dealing with Magic Johnson, so people are handling it with white gloves. They're not going to say how they really feel." Dr. Mellman told the press that it *might* be possible for players to contract HIV by bumping into Johnson, but the odds of doing so were "infinitesimally small." Nevertheless, all the controversy was too much for Johnson, who did not want to antagonize fellow players or cast a black cloud over the league. Nor did he, as a primary role model for HIV/AIDS patients, want to be viewed as a menace to society.

Thus, after playing five preseason games, Johnson announced his retirement on November 2. "It has become obvious that the various controversies surrounding my return are taking away from both basketball as a sport and the larger issue of living with HIV, for me and the many people affected," he said in a statement.

Despite his retirement, Johnson found it hard to stay away from the game. He was only 33 years old and remained one of the best players in the world. In 1993, he aimed to fulfill one of his longtime dreams: owning an NBA team. He was part of a group that wanted to buy the new NBA franchise in Toronto, but they lost out to another group.

In 1993, Johnson headed a touring team called Magic's Legends. Unfortunately, he was the only "legend" on the roster. Except for former All-Star Bob McAdoo, most of the players had been just solid NBA players, including Johnson's old Michigan State teammates Earl Cureton and Greg Kelser.

Magic's Legends played against teams of the Continental Basketball Association and in Europe, where Johnson was well-received.

All the while, Jerry Buss had his own plans for Johnson. Buss wanted him to coach the Lakers. Without Johnson leading the way, the Lakers had become just an ordinary club. In 1991-1992 and 1992-1993, they went a combined 82-82. After the Lakers started the 1993-1994 season at 27-37, Buss fired head coach Randy Pfund and convinced Johnson to coach the team.

Although Johnson tried his best, he was not cut out for coaching. He won just five of his 16 games before announcing his resignation at season's end. For Johnson, coaching had been too stressful. "I was in what my wife calls 'basketball mood,'" he said, as reported in the *Los Angeles Daily News.* "That means I'm crazy and I'm moody. She'll be talking to me, and I'm staring into space because I'm thinking about a play or I'm thinking about what we did last night."

Johnson began to pursue business interests, including a purchase of 5 percent of the Lakers franchise. Yet by late 1995—four years after contracting HIV—he still yearned to play in the NBA. "They said playing basketball would kill me," he said, as reported in *Time.* "Well, *not* playing basketball was killing me."

Magic was 27 pounds heavier than in 1991, and he would have to play forward because of his decline in quickness. On January 30, 1996, he made a triumphant return to the Lakers. When Johnson checked into that first game—wearing his Magic Johnson MVP sneakers—he received a standing ovation from the Forum crowd. "Magic's Back," read a sign in the crowd. Playing only about half the game, he rang up 19 points, 10 assists, and eight rebounds in a Lakers victory. "I can't even begin to tell you how I feel," Magic said after the game. "It was one of the most exciting days of my life. Ever. I never thought I would be here again, especially after the last time I retired. But tonight I had so much fun."

Johnson played remarkably well in his 32 games that season. While playing 29.9 minutes per game—the fewest of his career—he averaged 14.6 points, 6.9 assists, and 5.7 rebounds. Though just 24-18 before Johnson joined the team, the Lakers went 29-11 with the "old man" on the roster. Only a first-round exit in the playoffs tarnished his sensational comeback season.

After the playoffs, Johnson announced his third and final retirement. The reason was a bit surprising: he left the NBA not because he was too old, or that he was too ill to play, or because of a phobia against HIV-infected participants. He left because the game had changed. The NBA's young players, he believed, were too self-centered. "The Michael Jordans and the Larry Birds, the Dr. Js and the Kareems enabled them to make this kind of money because they drove the [TV] ratings up," he said, as reported by the Associated Press. "But they think because they're out in the NBA, they deserve all this money, and that's all they're concerned with.

"I'm a guy that just wants to win."

Magic Johnson had proved to be a winner time and time again, even while living with HIV. At age 36, he was about to begin another winning chapter in his extraordinary life.

8

A Whole Lot to Live For

In 1996, five years after Magic Johnson announced that he had HIV, *USA Today* updated America on his condition. In short, he was as good as ever. "He's healthy and vibrant and active," said Lakers general manager Jerry West.

As the father of Andre and two young children, Earvin III and an adopted daughter named Elisa, Magic Johnson had a whole lot to live for. "I want to walk my daughter down the aisle and give her away to somebody some day," he later told CNN. "I want to make sure I am still here to make sure my two young sons become men."

At the time, most HIV patients were living 8 to 11 years before developing symptoms of the disease. Some people were living longer than that, and Johnson was doing all he could to extend his life. He went to the gym five days a week at The Sports Club L.A., where he worked out and played basketball from 7:30 to 11:00 A.M. He took his medication, of course, and he lived as healthy as possible. "My diet is mostly chicken and fish," he told CNN. "I make sure I get a lot of vegetables, a lot of fruit. I am a big fruit man [and] vegetable man.... And I also get a lot of rest. That's the key. I may be up early, but I'm in bed early, too."

Many people with HIV withdraw from society. Not Johnson. He was out and about every day, greeting his buddies with handshakes and hugs. For him, HIV was like the Boston Celtics—a nemesis that he was determined to beat. "One thing that has helped me is my competitive attitude," Johnson told the *Los Angeles Times*. "I've always enjoyed challenges. I never, ever accept losing. That's why I think I'm doing well. That and my family and God."

Johnson continued to carry the torch for people with HIV and AIDS. In 1999, he was the main speaker for the United Nations World AIDS Day Conference. In 2003, he teamed up with U.S. House of Representatives Democratic leader Nancy Pelosi to support more federal funding for the AIDS Drug Assistance Program. The ADAP funded domestic programs that offered medications to low-income AIDS patients. "There are so many people out there that are trying to take care of themselves," Johnson told the media that day. "All they need is help getting what they need to live long, productive lives. That is why I am here."

According to his doctors' initial projections, Johnson should have been dead or dying by 2003. But improved medications, his healthy lifestyle, and, undoubtedly, his winning attitude have kept him alive and well. Throughout his illness, he never stopped giving. That summer, he hosted the Magic Johnson Sports Star Award Dinner & Auction. The annual event had helped raise more than $1.5 million for the Muscular Dystrophy Association.

Johnson also served as a United Nations Messenger of Peace, speaking to young people about drugs, violence, and other social issues. His smile still lights up the room, and his enthusiasm and can-do attitude are infectious. After listening to Johnson, many kids leave with a skip in their step, ready to improve their lives and take on the world.

URBAN INVESTMENTS

Johnson has also brought his winning touch to the business world. According to a 2008 *Los Angeles Times* story, he had accumulated about $700 million in business holdings and had a personal net worth of about $500 million. As a boy, he had fantasized about starring in basketball and becoming a rich businessman, but in both regards he has exceeded his wildest dreams. Along with Tiger Woods, Johnson might be the most successful athlete-businessperson in history.

Early in his business career, Johnson fell on his face—just as he had during the warm-up before his first NBA game. In 1992, he opened a sporting goods store in Baldwin Hills, California. The store failed, however, because he had not catered to the tastes of his young consumers. "I lost $200,000 because I was messing around and buying everything an old man liked," he said, as reported in the *Los Angeles Times*.

Learning from his mistakes, Johnson blazed a winning path in the business world. His name alone helped tremendously; after all, who wouldn't want to partner with the ultimate winner, Magic Johnson? Nevertheless, he would not have become enormously wealthy without his sharp mind and strong work ethic.

And as he did on the court, he also had great vision in the business world. Back in the mid-1990s, Johnson wanted to open businesses in economically depressed urban areas. At the time, corporations steered clear of investing in such areas. They felt that if the people in the area were poor, they would not have the money to shop at the stores. Moreover, the high crime rate often prevelant in such areas meant that business owners would have to pay high insurance rates. Many investors did not want their employees to be in danger or their stores to be vandalized. It was a safer bet to invest in the suburbs or wealthier sections of the city.

Johnson, though, had faith in the "bad" neighborhoods. He believed that those in "the 'hood" had at least some buying power and that they were lacking in such establishments as restaurants and movie theaters. When he approached potential business partners, however, he found that they did not share his vision. "A lot of them wanted my autograph and a picture with me," he said in the *Los Angeles Times* article. "But they didn't want to invest with me. People said, 'If you believe in urban America so much, why don't you invest your money and prove it?'"

So Johnson did just that. His Johnson Development Corporation teamed with Sony-Loews Theatres to open the first Magic Johnson Theatre in 1995. Finally, residents of the Baldwin Hills district of Los Angeles could watch movies in style. Over time, Johnson and his partners opened more Magic Johnson Theatres, in Los Angeles and other big cities, including the Harlem neighborhood of New York. To maximize the number of customers, Johnson "Magicized" his theaters. That is, he altered the refreshment stands to meet the tastes of his urban customers. For example, he added spicy hot dogs and Buffalo wings to the concession stands.

In 1995, Johnson wanted to establish other businesses in urban neighborhoods. The California Public Employees' Retirement System (CalPERS) invested $50 million in his ventures—then added another $100 million. His alliance with Canyon Capital in 1998 provided him with even more money to invest.

Earvin's corporation, Magic Johnson Enterprises, became a financial empire. Today, the corporation has a stake in not just movie theaters but more than 30 Burger Kings and more than 100 Starbucks. Patrons can burn off their calories at more than a dozen Magic Johnson Sport Clubs. Johnson also has invested in a TGI Friday's, a Best Buy, and other businesses.

Magic Johnson speaks at the opening of a new Sherman Oaks Magic Johnson Sport Club in Los Angeles on May 9, 2002. Because of his reputation as a philanthropist, businessman, and AIDS activist, pundits often say Johnson would make a formidable political candidate.

"My strength is urban America," Johnson told *USA Today*, and he proved it over and over again. His businesses were so profitable that investors clamored to invest in his company. In 2008, Magic Johnson Enterprises had raised, but had yet to deploy, $1 billion.

Again, "Magicizing" played a key role. At the first Starbucks that he opened in Los Angeles, he added picnic tables outside. The tables attracted the many chess players in the neighborhood, who gave the place a welcoming feel. At many of his urban Starbucks, he played R&B music and added sweet potato pie to the dessert menu. Also, if you go to the drive-through at one of Johnson's Burger Kings, you're greeted by a recording of Magic's voice.

In 2008, Johnson wrote a book titled *32 Ways to Be a Champion in Business*. The number 32 (his jersey number) was more than just a gimmick. He provided 32 sage business lessons, such as "Think of your employees as fellow entrepreneurs" and "Focus on the customer and you will never go wrong."

Johnson insists that the key to his success was investing in underdeveloped urban areas and understanding the needs of the people in those areas. In an interview on his official Web site, MagicJohnson.com, he said:

> I remember at my TGI Friday's grand opening, an older woman came up to me, hugged me, and said, "I've lived here for 25 years and until today, I've never been able to eat a salad at a restaurant in my own community, so thank you." . . . It's been extremely rewarding to know that I've impacted the growth and development of cities across the country and have found a way to bring the pride back into communities.

EVER EVOLVING

Johnson has been criticized for investing in fast-food restaurants. With obesity and diabetes on the rise in urban areas, he realizes that "I've got to get urban America healthier."

"If we're going to move urban America forward," he continued at an environmental conference in Irvine, California, in 2009, "we need to have the information tools you have. If you say organic, most of our kids don't know what you are talking about, because they haven't been taught that."

In recent years, Johnson has used his clout in politics. In 2008, he endorsed Senator Hillary Clinton of New York for president of the United States. But after she lost in the Democratic primaries, he had no qualms about supporting the Democratic nominee, Senator Barack Obama of Illinois. In fact, when Obama won the election in November, Magic and Cookie Johnson "jumped up for joy, we were hollering and screaming," he said, as reported by the Associated Press. "And then we started crying. As African Americans, we've made great strides."

Johnson likes President Obama's qualities. "He's a motivator," he said about Obama in the Associated Press article. "He has a plan. One thing Barack can do, he can come in a room, command a room. Everyone will listen to every word."

LIVING WITH HIV

Despite all of his accomplishments since 1991, Johnson cannot fully shake the stigma: He's the guy with HIV. Since he contracted the disease, confusion, ignorance, and myths have surrounded his condition.

At first, millions of people thought he had AIDS and that he was dying. Once they learned that he had HIV, they still figured that he had only a few years left to live. At first, even doctors believed he probably wouldn't survive more than 10 years. By 2009, after living 18 years with HIV, Johnson still seemed perfectly healthy. Why?

In October 2008, two Minneapolis radio hosts thought they had the answer: Johnson had faked getting HIV, they said. The hosts' reckless assertion was false, of course, and it angered Johnson and his loved ones. "We can't have people out here making false statements and putting out bad information, because this battle is too big when it comes to HIV and AIDS," Johnson told the Associated Press. "I poured my life into it and a lot of other people have poured their life into it, into getting out the right information so people can protect themselves and know what HIV and AIDS is all about." When asked if he thought the hosts should be fired, Johnson took the high ground. "I would rather they educate their audience," he told the Associated Press reporter.

Magic Johnson neither faked his illness, nor is he dying. And HIV did not disappear from his body—another false rumor. Johnson has lived this long because he has taken good care of himself and—most importantly—because scientists have made great strides in drug therapy for HIV patients.

In 1993, the estimated life expectancy for a symptom-less HIV-infected person was less than seven years. In 2006, the life expectancy for such a person was 24 years. According to

Magic Among the Greats

According to a panel of experts put together by the Associated Press, Magic Johnson was the fifth-greatest basketball player of the twentieth century. It was hard to argue with the men ahead of him:

- Michael Jordan (ranked No. 1) won 10 NBA scoring titles and six NBA championships with the Chicago Bulls.

- Wilt Chamberlain (No. 2) averaged 30.1 points and 22.9 rebounds per game for his career.

- Oscar Robertson (No. 3) averaged 25.7 PPG compared to Magic's 19.5. The Big O's 9.5 APG and 7.5 RPG compare to Johnson's 11.2 APG and 7.2 RPG.

- Bill Russell (No. 4) tallied 22.5 rebounds per game for his career. He led Boston to 11 NBA championships and has been called the greatest defensive player of all time.

The Associated Press experts placed Johnson fifth on the list for leading the Lakers to five NBA championships, winning three NBA MVP Awards, and setting the NBA record for career assists. Following Johnson were, in order, his rival Larry Bird, teammate Kareem Abdul-Jabbar, old-time Lakers Elgin Baylor and Jerry West, and Philadelphia 76ers legend Julius Erving. In 2003, the editors at *Slam*, a well-respected basketball magazine, also ranked the greatest NBA players of all time. Their top five were the same as the Associated Press's, except they put Russell ahead of Robertson.

Most experts pick Johnson as the best point guard of all time, ahead of such legends as John Stockton and Bob Cousy. In 2007, *Sports Illustrated*'s Ian Thomsen selected his all-time dream team. Thomsen stirred controversy with his starting frontcourt: Bill Russell, Tim Duncan, and Larry Bird. But few could argue with his all-time backcourt: Michael Jordan at shooting guard and Magic Johnson at the point.

the Associated Press, "since the mid-1990s, about two dozen HIV-fighting antiretroviral drugs have come onto the market that have essentially turned HIV from a death sentence into a chronic disease."

Unfortunately, proper medications and care cost the average HIV patient about $25,000 per year. The government and organizations help defray the cost, but certainly not all HIV patients receive proper care. Johnson, of course, can afford the finest care possible. In 2008, he said his health was "wonderful," and he hopes that he will greatly exceed the average 24-year expectancy. He also hopes that the average life expectancy for HIV patients will continue to increase—perhaps to 30 years or more.

Day after day, scientists work relentlessly to find a cure for HIV. Although there is no sure cure at present, researchers continue to take positive steps. For example, the World Health Organization is studying whether to put all HIV patients in certain countries or regions on antiretroviral-drug therapy. The therapy not only helps people like Johnson live longer, but those on the therapy almost never pass HIV to other people. In theory, if every HIV patient in America and across the world took antiretroviral-drug therapy, then future generations would be virtually HIV-free.

Scientists have made other breakthroughs, as well. For instance, they are making progress in their efforts to genetically engineer a patient's cells to make them HIV resistant. And in 2009, *The New England Journal of Medicine* reported on a 42-year-old HIV patient in Germany. After receiving a bone-marrow transplant for leukemia, he no longer had any evidence of HIV in his body. Such stories put hope in the hearts of HIV patients, including Magic Johnson.

THE GREATEST

Magic Johnson takes his business and philanthropic work seriously, but he also loves to have a good time. He has served as an NBA analyst for TNT and, recently, for ESPN and ABC. In

A girl sits at a computer as Magic Johnson looks over her shoulder at the Mattie Koonce Learning Center in Miami, Florida, on February 20, 2004. Through his foundation, Johnson helped donate $200,000 in computer equipment to the learning center. It was the twelfth Magic Johnson HP Inventor Center to open in an inner-city community.

1998, he hosted a late-night talk show on Fox called *The Magic Hour*. Unfortunately, the title was the best part of the show, which the critics panned. Nevertheless, he enjoyed himself even if the viewers did not. As a reporter for the *Washington Post* put it, "Johnson laughed himself dopey but failed equally to amuse the audience."

Though talk shows might not have been be his forte, Johnson has lived an extraordinarily successful life. Time and again, he has made a profound impact on the world. His charisma and dynamic play increased national enthusiasm for the NCAA Tournament. His "winning time" success with the Showtime Lakers spurred international interest in the NBA. Johnson has served as an ambassador for HIV patients, raising awareness of the disease and generating compassion for the suffering individuals.

In addition, he has created a whole new business model, one that invested in inner cities and put faith in underserved communities. Along the way, he became one of the wealthiest black businesspeople in the United States. The Magic Johnson Foundation has raised millions of dollars for worthy causes, and his motivational speeches have inspired thousands of young people to improve their lives and the world.

Incredibly, Johnson achieved his basketball success at a remarkably young age (high school, NCAA, and NBA championships by age 20), and he built his financial empire while battling a life-threatening disease. As an African American from a working-class family, he overcame societal obstacles, as well. As Johnson himself has said, nobody from *his* neighborhood had ever become famous.

Magic Johnson became hugely famous—a larger-than-life figure. In 1999, ESPN rated Johnson as the seventeenth-greatest athlete of the twentieth century, just two spots below the immortal Jackie Robinson. Yet "athlete" only partly defines Johnson, a person of enormous gifts. Wrote Jack Kroll of *Newsweek*, "The great appeal of Magic is that he packs human virtues into Olympian size." Perhaps one of the best compliments paid to Johnson came from his old archrival and good friend Larry Bird. "Every time I see him," Bird said, "I'm happier."

And that, in a nutshell, describes the magic of Earvin Johnson.

1959 Earvin Johnson Jr. is born on August 14 in Lansing, Michigan.

1979 Johnson leads Michigan State to a 75-64 triumph over Indiana State and Larry Bird in the most-watched NCAA championship game of all time. He is selected by the Los Angeles Lakers as the first overall pick in the NBA Draft.

1980 On May 16, Johnson scores 42 points in Game 6 of the NBA Finals against Philadelphia to clinch the championship. Though a rookie, he is named the NBA Finals MVP.

1982 He earns the NBA Finals MVP Award after leading the Lakers over Philadelphia.

1983 Johnson leads the NBA in assists (10.5) for the first time and makes the All-NBA First Team for the first of nine straight seasons. His first autobiography, *Magic*, written with Richard Levin, is published.

1985 On June 9, he powers the Lakers to victory over Larry Bird's Boston Celtics in the decisive Game 6 of the NBA Finals.

1986 In February, Johnson becomes the first player to receive more than a million votes in balloting for the NBA All-Star Game.

1987 He wins his first NBA MVP Award after averaging 23.9 points and 12.2 assists per game. He is named the NBA Finals MVP after leading the Lakers over the Celtics in the championship series.

1988 On June 21, he wins his fifth NBA championship with the Lakers when they defeat the Detroit Pistons in Game 7 of the NBA Finals.

1989 Johnson is named NBA MVP after leading the Lakers to their eighth straight Pacific Division title.

1990 He wins his third NBA MVP Award after leading the Lakers to a 63-19 record.

1991 On April 15, Johnson records his 9,888th career assist, breaking Oscar Robertson's NBA record. On November 7, he announces that he tested positive for HIV and will retire as an NBA player. That same month, President George H.W. Bush names him to the National Commission on AIDS.

1992 Johnson plays in the NBA All-Star Game and wins the game's MVP Award. His book *What You Can Do to Avoid AIDS* is published. *A Conversation with Magic Johnson*, about sex and HIV, airs on Nickelodeon and public television. In August, he wins an Olympic gold medal as part of the U.S. "Dream Team." On September 29, he announces that he will return to the Lakers, although a backlash by some NBA players will prompt him to change his mind. His second autobiography, *My Life*, written with William Novak, is published.

1994 Johnson becomes head coach of the Lakers. He steps down after the season.

1995 The first Magic Johnson Theatre opens in Los Angeles.

1996 Johnson returns to the Lakers as a player. He retires after the season.

2002 He is elected to the Naismith Memorial Basketball Hall of Fame.

2008 Johnson's book *32 Ways to Be a Champion in Business* is published.

2009 *When the Game Was Ours*, a book coauthored by Johnson, Larry Bird, and Jackie MacMullen, is published.

Further Reading

Bird, Larry, and Earvin "Magic" Johnson, with Jackie MacMullen. *When the Game Was Ours.* Boston: Houghton Mifflin Harcourt, 2009.

Blatt, Howard. *Magic! Against the Odds.* New York: Pocket Books, 1996.

Davis, Seth. *When March Went Mad: The Game That Transformed Basketball.* New York: Times Books, 2009.

Gottfried, Ted. *Earvin Magic Johnson: Champion and Crusader.* New York: Franklin Watts, 2001.

Gutman, Bill. *Magic, More Than a Legend.* New York: Harper Paperbacks, 1992.

Johnson, Earvin, and Richard Levin. *Magic.* New York: Viking Press, 1983.

Johnson, Earvin "Magic." *Magic's Touch: From Fundamentals to Fast Break With One of Basketball's All-Time Greats.* Reading, Mass.: Addison-Wesley, 1992.

———. *What You Can Do to Avoid AIDS.* New York: Three Rivers Press, 1996.

———. *32 Ways to Be a Champion in Business.* New York: Crown Business, 2008.

Johnson, Earvin "Magic," and William Novak. *My Life.* New York: Random House, 1992.

Lazenby, Roland. *The Show: The Inside Story of the Spectacular Los Angeles Lakers in the Words of Those Who Lived It.* New York: McGraw-Hill, 2005.

Los Angeles Times Sports Staff. *The Los Angeles Lakers: 50 Amazing Years in the City of Angels.* San Francisco: Time Capsule Press, 2009.

Pascarelli, Peter. *The Courage of Magic Johnson: From Boyhood Dreams to Superstar to His Toughest Challenge.* New York: Bantam Books, 1992.

Riley, Pat. *The Winner Within: A Life Plan for Team Players.* New York: Warner Books, 1988.

Ross, Alan. *Lakers Glory: For the Love of Kobe, Magic, and Mikan.* Nashville: Cumberland House, 2006.

Schwabacher, Martin. *Magic Johnson.* New York: Chelsea House, 1993.

WEB SITES
AIDS.org
http://www.aids.org/

Basketball-Reference.com
http://www.basketball-reference.com/players/j/johnsma02.html

Magic Johnson Enterprises
http://www.magicjohnson.org/

NBA.com (Magic Johnson page)
http://www.nba.com/history/players/johnsonm_bio.html

NBA.com (Los Angeles Lakers page)
http://www.nba.com/lakers/

Picture Credits

page

2: Mark J. Terrill/AP Images

5: Al Behrman/AP Images

13: J. Walter Green/AP Images

15: FHJ/AP Images

22: RMK/AP Images

27: Brian Horton/AP Images

29: AP Images

34: Marty Lederhandler/AP Images

36: Randy Rasmussen/AP Images

39: Marty Lederhandler/AP Images

48: Peter Southwick/AP Images

53: © Steve Lipofsky/Corbis

65: © Bettmann/CORBIS

70: © TRAPPER FRANK/ CORBIS SYGMA

75: Werner Slocum/AP Images

78: Dennis Cook/AP Images

85: © Gregg Newton/Corbis

93: Mark J. Terrill/AP Images

98: William Torres/AP Images

Index

About the Author

David Aretha grew up in Michigan, where he watched Magic Johnson defeat his high school's basketball team at the 1977 state championship game. Aretha has written and edited dozens of sports books. He is the editor of *Basketball Legends of All Time*, *The Michael Jordan Scrapbook*, and the annual *Basketball Almanac*. In addition, he cowrote *Raging Bulls: NBA Champs* and authored books for young readers on the Detroit Pistons and Seattle SuperSonics.